Eufeeling!

ALSO BY DR. FRANK J. KINSLOW

The Secret of Instant Healing

The Secret of Quantum Living

Beyond Happiness:
Finding and Fulfilling Your Deepest Desire
(available January 2013)

All of the above are available at your local bookstore,
or may be ordered by visiting:

Hay House USA: **www.hayhouse.com**®
Hay House Australia: **www.hayhouse.com.au**
Hay House UK: **www.hayhouse.co.uk**
Hay House South Africa: **www.hayhouse.co.za**
Hay House India: **www.hayhouse.co.in**

Eufeeling!

The Art of Creating
Inner Peace and Outer Prosperity

DR. FRANK J. KINSLOW

HAY HOUSE, INC.
Carlsbad, California • New York City
London • Sydney • Johannesburg
Vancouver • Hong Kong • New Delhi

Published and distributed in the United States by: Hay House, Inc.: www.hayhouse.com® • **Published and distributed in Australia by:** Hay House Australia Pty. Ltd.: www.hayhouse.com.au • **Published and distributed in the United Kingdom by:** Hay House UK, Ltd.: www.hayhouse.co.uk • **Published and distributed in the Republic of South Africa by:** Hay House SA (Pty), Ltd.: www.hayhouse.co.za • **Distributed in Canada by:** Raincoast: www.raincoast.com • **Published in India by:** Hay House Publishers India: www.hayhouse.co.in

Cover design: Julie Davison • *Interior design:* Pamela Homan
Interior illustrations: Courtesy of the author

Quantum Entrainment® is a registered trademark of Frank Kinslow and VAK Verlags GmbH, Germany. QE™, Eufeeling™, and QE Intention™ are unregistered trademarks of Frank Kinslow and VAK Verlags GmbH, Germany. All trademarks may only be used with permission. © 2010 Quantum Entrainment. All rights reserved.

Library of Congress Cataloging-in-Publication Data

Kinslow, Frank J.
  Eufeeling! : the art of creating inner peace and outer prosperity / Frank J. Kinslow. -- 1st ed.
    p. cm.
  ISBN 978-1-4019-3399-9 (tradepaper : alk. paper) 1. Mind and body. 2. Awareness. 3. Healing. 4. New Thought. I. Title.
  BF161.K558 2012
  158.1--dc23
                                              2012004743

Tradepaper ISBN: 978-1-4019-3399-9
Digital ISBN: 978-1-4019-3400-2

15 14 13 12   4 3 2 1
1st edition, July 2012

Printed in the United States of America

In recognition of all you Transcenders out there . . .

you know who you are.

Contents

Preface

This book is written for both the first-time reader and those who are already familiar with the Quantum Entrainment® (QE™) process. If you were introduced to QE through one of my previous books, you will find some familiar material in the early part of this book. This is unavoidable if we make available to new readers the wonders of this unique and effective technology and show them how to integrate it into their lives. However, I feel that even the most seasoned Quantum Entrainment practitioner (QE'er) will find that the new experiences, analogies, and insights more than make up for any repetition of QE concepts.

The second part of this book will introduce you to QE Intention. QE Intention is a powerful new technology founded on an obscure, almost secret teaching that was first practiced over 4,000 years ago in ancient India. In Sanskrit, it is called Ritam Bhara Pragya, which elicits a level of awareness that perceives with absolute clarity the seeds of creation. But don't let that befuddle you. QE Intention is easy and natural and can be done by anyone. It shows you how to easily take the consciousness you are using to read these lines and use it to plant your own seeds for better health, fulfilling relationships, financial security, or whatever it is that you desire in your life. QE Intention can be applied by anyone, in any situation, and is a powerful addition to those who are already doing intention work.

Whether you are a seasoned QE'er or an enthusiastic first-time reader, this book promises to provide you with new insights and practices to make your life more vibrant, fulfilling, and fun. Thanks for joining us and welcome aboard.

Love & Laughter,

Frank Kinslow
Sarasota, Florida

CHAPTER 1

The Point

"Great doubt will eventually lead to great awakening."

— HAN YONGUN

Experience: Tip of Tongue

Gently place the tip of your tongue precisely on the ridge where your gums meet your upper front teeth. Place it easily against the ridge and pay close attention to everything you can feel where the tip of your tongue touches your teeth and gums. Just be quietly aware of what you feel there.

Which is smoother: your tongue, your gums, or your teeth? Which is rougher? Which is cooler? Become aware of the saliva between your tongue, teeth, and gums. Now, pay attention to how much pressure your tongue is exerting against your teeth and gums. Can you feel the muscles in your tongue? Is your tongue relaxed? For 15 or 20 seconds, become very clearly aware of everything you can feel where your tongue touches your teeth and gums.

Now, become aware of how you generally feel throughout your body. Notice that your body is more relaxed now than before you first put your tongue against your teeth and gums. Also note that your mind is more alert and at the same time more peaceful. How can this be? How can the innocent act of paying attention to a single point within your mouth create a more relaxed body and a clearer, more peaceful mind? When you answer this question, you will unlock the secret to health, harmony, and material abundance in your life.

That is why I am writing to you. You have everything you need with you, right now. Whether you know it or not, sitting right where you are, holding this book in your hands, you are poised for perfection. Just as the Tip of Tongue experience above opened you to greater harmony in body and mind, you are at a point in your life that will just as effortlessly take you beyond the bonds of boredom, struggle, and strife to experience the frictionless flow of wealth and wellness. Anyone can become aware of their teeth and tongue, millions do so every day, but not everyone does it in a way that increases body-mind harmony as you did just a few moments ago. They are capable, they have everything they need, but they just aren't aware of this simple process that improves body-mind unity in seconds.

You are at a unique point in your life, both literally and figuratively. You can literally alter the course of your life without leaving the chair you are sitting in. From that vantage point, this book will open your awareness to treasures within you, yearning to be discovered. This simple book is your treasure map. Just like the Tip of Tongue exercise, this book will lead you step by step. It will show you where to find the precious jewels of peace, prosperity, and joyful living free of conflict that await just on the other side of your mind.

"Sure," you say, "I felt more peace and relaxation after I did the exercise. But I have financial concerns, and I have a troublesome relationship. How is becoming aware of my tongue and teeth going to pay my rent and smooth out the edges of a rocky relationship?"

Stepping Outside Your Mind

Great question. I'm glad you asked. The secret is not in the tongue but how our minds become conscious of it. At least the mind is our starting point. For it is the mind that is the troublemaker. So, we first take a look at how our minds make mischief. Then we will learn how to reach beyond our minds for the solution. You see, we have been led astray, misdirected. We have been bamboozled into thinking that we could use our minds to fix our minds. That's like asking a thief for suggestions on where to safely hide your money. We can't expect a broken mind to fix itself. That is a very special kind of insanity that has wormed its way into every expression of our lives, and we are suffering because of it.

What is needed is a way to step outside of the mind, take a look around, and then step back into our mind fully aware. The difference between the rest and peace you got from the Tip of Tongue exercise and someone who doesn't participate in the exercise is simply awareness. We need to look at ourselves and our lives from a vantage point beyond the manipulative influence of our mind. We need to be free of the impact of damaging emotions, prejudice, slanted logic, and misinformation that sways our every thought, word, and action. We do this with a very specialized awareness that we all have but seldom make use of. This book will show you how to unfold this awareness in your life. It will not require your belief, for it is beyond belief. You will be taught a scientific technique that will let you slip beyond the grasp of common consciousness into a super-conscious state as effortlessly and naturally as breathing. This awareness by itself has remarkable rejuvenating and re-storative power for body and mind, but there is more.

Once you learn to step outside your mind, you will learn how to step back inside with a new perspective. Instead of your mind controlling you, you will be in control of your mind. Or, more accurately, you will be aware of how your mind has fooled you into thinking that your life is a struggle. With new clarity, you will watch as those distortions innately mend themselves. The whole process is most extraordinary. But there is still more.

Once you become comfortable with your newfound inner awareness, it will be time to learn to use it to bet-ter your outer life. That's right, you will learn to fulfill desires both on the inner emotional and outer material planes. Now is your time to learn to fulfill your deepest desires and even your most frivolous ones. You will learn to satisfy both elements of the desire complex. You will learn how to quell destructive emotional attachments immediately, and from that placid point of being, you will watch as the forces of physics gather to bring to you the very thing you desired on the physical plane.

What do you say? Do you think it's worth a little more of your time to learn how to transcend the prob-lems that plague your life? Are you ready to use your body-mind the way it was intended, to make life easier for not only you but your friends, family, and the rest of us who share this planet with you? Well, don't get up. Stay right where you are, and let everything unfold through the prevailing forces of fulfillment. Learn to see with fresh eyes the harmony within the human condition. Come to know the perfection of the present as a perception that is open to all humankind. Otherwise, what's the point?

Main Points for Chapter 1

- Paying attention in just the right way increases body-mind harmony.

- We can't use a broken mind to fix itself.

- Stepping outside of the mind frees us of damaging emotions, prejudice, slanted logic, and misinformation that sways our every thought, word, and action.

- Fulfilling desires is easy with a clear, unobstructed mind.

- You can transform your world without leaving the chair you are sitting in.

CHAPTER 2

Finding Our Way Back Home

"It is utterly false and cruelly arbitrary to put all the play and learning into childhood, all the work into middle age, and all the regrets into old age."

— MARGARET MEAD

The Magic Years

Do you remember the magic of being a child? Do you remember when your best friend was a stuffed animal that you trusted and loved with all your heart? You could play self-absorbed for hours with your toddler-sized tea set, splashing in puddles in your new red rain boots, or squealing at the funny sensation in your stomach from swinging way, way high, up in the sky. All the while, you were continually wrapped in awe of even the most ordinary objects and events. An ant on an apple core, dew on a spiderweb, brightly colored veins in a broken rock: no matter what activity drew your attention, you were completely absorbed in peace and joy and inner contentment. You were just being you, and it felt marvelous.

How often do you recapture the joy of being fully human today? Have you pushed those memories into the dusty basement of your adult mind? If you revisited them now, would you find only broken images of your youth scattered on a shelf around a forgotten tea set?

You cannot recapture your childhood, but you can recapture the joy and excitement that was its common companion. You have not abandoned it, and it has not abandoned you. The love that animated your childhood still dwells within you. That is what I want to tell you. That is why I am writing to you. Somewhere along the way, stuffed animals and red rain boots were traded for educational goals, job security, and respectability in the community, all somehow lacking the spontaneous beauty of those innocent, magic years. But they are just a heartbeat or two away from where you are living right now.

The wonder of life is not uniquely a childhood phenomenon. You may have had fleeting glimpses of the awe inherent in the human condition when you gazed deeply into the blackness of a star-strewn sky or felt the helplessness of a newborn child as she lay breathing with soft, pink puffs at her mother's breast. Joy and love and peace are there for the taking. It is only that you have momentarily turned your attention to the more *important* things in life. The good news is your return to childhood does not require discarding what you have earned as an adult. On the contrary, you can have your cake and eat it too. When you have the right recipe, the methodical motions of adulthood are infinitely enhanced by the spontaneity that characterized your childhood.

We do not have to choose one over the other. We do not have to lament the loss of inner joys for outer security. We commonly misunderstand adulthood. The problem is we stop growing too soon. You see, what we normally express as adult behavior is still abysmally immature.

Adulthood as we know it today is really more like extended adolescence. An adolescent thinks he is more grown up than experience or aptitude can support. For this reason, juveniles are disruptive, and many times dangerous to themselves and others. If you think about it, most adults are even more disruptive and dangerous. We have more power to pollute and pillage in the name of progress. It takes only a moment's reflection to recognize that our species is perilously close to extinction because of destructive behavior by *adults* on every level of society the world over.

There is more to human development than we have been living. Innately, we know that there must be something more to life. Maybe you have asked yourself that very question in a time of quiet desperation. It usually comes in midlife, when we have acquired most of the things we desired, and still we feel an intangible emptiness, an inner incompleteness. The voice, no more than a gentle ripple across the ocean of our mind, issues from that strange, still place deep inside. We listen closely, for we know it is trying to tell us something important. But it is a frail voice drowned out by the wind and waves of daily living. And so we go on forging the life that our forefathers dreamed for us, the life of dominion over our environment, a life that ultimately reflects opulence, power, and pride.

Generally, we recognize childhood, adolescence, and adulthood as the major stages of human growth. We expect to move steadily through these phases, gathering to us more education, wealth, and power. We expect to find happiness like the fabled pot of gold at the end of the rainbow of our lives. In the end, what is cherished most are memories. Even the richest and most powerful among us fall back on our memories in the end. It is as if we realize altogether too late that outer rewards pale in the presence of the real power, the times in our lives of compassion, camaraderie, and love.

This has been the lament of the human race for a single reason. We settle for the hope of lasting happiness, which always seems to be just beyond our grasp. The happiness we do manage to snatch is fleeting and leaves us yearning for more. Happiness in all its guises—relationships, sex, money, and more—is a phantom of reality. Once achieved, it has no substance, no lasting value to give us what we really yearn for. That will only come with a clear and innocent perception of our true reality. The truth is that we are only living half a life. We have not yet slipped into our spiritual skin. We have not grown into our full potential as dynamic, fun-loving paragons of peace and propriety.

I am not talking about evolution here. We were born with everything we need to be free of the destructive tendencies of the immature adult. We already know that we are capable of great acts of kindness, love, and charity. In fact, we hold these attributes and others like them as the epitome of humanness. What I am suggesting is not evolution but revolution; that is, if revolution means finally living up to what it is to be fully human.

I don't think there are many who would argue that we are capable of far more harmony and healing than we are presently exhibiting. And I know that you are probably thinking that we have been trying to elevate ourselves above our destructive tendencies since the first caveman bonked his neighbor on the head with a club and stole his woman. I am not suggesting we try to overcome destructive tendencies. Nor am I suggesting that we try to neutralize them with positive thoughts or actions. We have pursued both paths with little lasting success. I am suggesting that we don't try anything. In fact, trying will only make it worse.

Left on its own, a child will perish. Left to his own devices, it appears that the adult imposes his own brand of fatality on the world. It is clear that we must find a solution that can combine the innocence and exuberance of childhood with the wisdom and proficiency of adulthood: a coming together of the heart and the head. But does such a solution exist? Yes! Of course it does. Otherwise, this would be a very short book indeed.

Return to Grace

You can look at it like completing the circle. Or in terms of Milton's *Paradise Lost,* after falling from grace, we return to the exalted state of original innocence but with a single and very important difference. When we return to claim the innocence of childhood we are experienced, tainted if you will, by the harshness of the world. Such a person has suffered and then transcended the self-indulgence of both the inner child and outer adult worlds to integrate play and work, spontaneity and control, love and lust. This blending of the best of both worlds is done not with dedication and hard work or by evoking the divine favor of the gods. It is achieved simply through a shift in perception. The child in us knows it instinctively. The adult only need accept that it is true, right here, right now. That is the elegant truth. But how to make it true for us?

Here is an experience that can break through the rigid thinking that imprisons the adult mind.

Experience: Finding Your Eternal Self

Evoke an early memory from childhood, perhaps one where you were playing quietly by yourself or some other pleasant activity. Now, let your mind shift to an event later in your childhood. Choose events in adolescence, young adulthood, and continue to the present time. Let the memory become more vivid. Stay with each occurrence for as long as you like, remembering the sounds and smells, how your body felt, and what emotions were in your mind. When you finish with one memory, move to the next more recent memory.

After you have revisited several memories from different times in your life, let them all flow along in your mind at one time, like a river of memories. As you do, realize that you are observing your memories. It is like you are on the bank of the river, watching your memories flow by. Realize that at this moment you are the observer of what is occurring in your mind, in this case, your memories.

Go back to one of the single memory events you just had and remember it very clearly. As you watch your memory unfold, realize that during the actual event, while you were making the memory, you also had a part of you that was watching what you were doing. There was a part of you that was observing even then. Visit another memory and realize that you were actually observing during that event as well.

Now, take all the memories you chose earlier and watch them from beginning to end in quick succession. Note that your body, intellect, emotions, desires, and skills all changed as you aged from childhood to adulthood. But there was something that didn't change. The sense of I, the silent witnessing Self, was always there just as it is right now. Become conscious that you are aware of it, aware of this whole process going on right now. Become aware that you were aware then, and you are aware now. Know that there is nothing in that awareness but awareness: unchanging, undying awareness itself.

No matter what your body-mind is experiencing, there has always been the silent, eternal witness of your inner Self. That is the timeless You, the eternal Self, which will never leave you. How could it? You can leave your body and your mind, but you can never leave your Self.

Just the realization that there is *something* that is stable in our life has a very settling effect. We feel somehow more secure knowing that there is a part of us that does not decay. We may not know how to explain it or show it to others, but we know it is there, and that is enough for now. But don't worry; you will soon learn how to make this experience vivid and vibrant in your life. Let's look a little more closely at what it means to live in this heightened state of awareness.

Most of us live in Newton's land of laws, the goal-oriented land of cause and effect, convinced that when we perform X + Y we would certainly achieve the target result Z. That is, we are certain that getting an education and a good job while picking up a family, a house, and a dog along the way, we will amass sufficient security and wealth to live out the rest of our lives in relative ease and happiness. How many of us are exactly where we planned to be ten years ago? It's almost impossible to get exactly what you plan for in life. Life has other plans for us. We strive for what we want, but life gives us what we need. Life offers us viable alternatives to our journey, and if we resist, life offers us obstacles.

When I refer to *life* here, I am talking about the laws of nature to which we are all subservient. The laws that govern our species, our Earth, and even the vast worlds that revolve beyond our comprehension. And most of all, the law that underlies them all: the law of perfection through present perception. What does that mean? Don't let the words scare you off. It is quite straightforward. Present perception means becoming aware of pure awareness, a simple shift from common consciousness to unbounded awareness that anyone who is reading these lines can do effortlessly. It is the missing link that unites the freedom of childhood with the progressive power of adulthood. Bear with me a little longer, and I will not only explain how it works but how to win the favor of Mother Nature and live free from the binding influence of struggle and stress. Just know that when we bend or break the laws of nature, we will be reprimanded. In childhood, it is our mother who suggests, guides, and disciplines us. In adulthood, Mother Nature takes over the job. As we already know, she can be brutal and unrelenting or compassionate, loving, and generous. The decision is not hers but ours to make.

This is not just some fanciful, pie-in-the-sky philosophy. What I am saying is as tangible as the air you are breathing. We have many examples of those who have lived this elevated human existence. It is not a matter of learning something new but more of remembering: remembering what we are, remembering our very essence. It is like returning to the freedom of childhood while living within the confines of control-oriented adulthood. It is a coming together of childhood and adulthood to form a new, exciting compilation of the best of both lives. It is a kind of enlightenment, an opening to the quiet power that lies within each and every one of us.

The Perception of Perfection

This elevated state is not odd or out of reach. It is not foreign to us in any way. Quite the contrary; it is as natural as thinking. And it is just as easy to realize. That is because it is not something new to the human condition. Not at all. It is not a new way of thinking or behaving. It doesn't even require that you believe it will work. Under normal circumstances, when you cut your finger, in time it will heal. That is the natural response of your body. You do not have to will the cut to heal; nor do you have to believe that it will heal. Healing takes place automatically and without any effort on your part. Elevating yourself beyond the common experience of struggle and suffering is also completely natural. Once you know how to make the shift, your life will naturally radiate joy and peace and awe just as effortlessly and naturally as a cut finger heals.

This advanced state belongs to us as human beings and is the natural progression beyond our present condition of inner dissonance. How hard will it be for you to realize and live it in your own life? Not at all! In fact, when you follow this simple rule of observation, perfect perception will descend on you as fluidly as dawn descends on darkness. Once the shift takes place, you will ascend above the trouble and trauma of daily living in a way that is at the same time common and celestial. With your feet planted firmly on terra firma, your heart will open to the essence of humanity, while your inner vision opens to the completeness of creation.

You will find the perception of perfection is waiting for you at the furthest boundaries of your mind. Like a butterfly alighting on a luminescent petal, your awareness will softly settle on pure awareness. That is, if you know this simple rule, this law of perfection: There is nowhere to go; there is nothing to do. Obscured to the vision of the action-oriented mind, this edict of enlightenment will soon become a gentle reminder of the *other world* in which you live. Right now, it may be unknown to you. Your consciousness may most often be drawn to the fuss and fireworks of your everyday routine. We'll fix that. And we'll start right now by looking at what forces labor in your mind that work against the perception of perfection.

Main Points for Chapter 2

- The love that animated your childhood still dwells within you.

- Adulthood as we know it today is really more like extended adolescence.

- Happiness in all its guises—relationships, sex, money, and more—is a phantom of reality.

- We are capable of far more harmony and healing than we presently exhibit.

- Your inner Self is eternal and unchanging.

- Experiencing what it is to be fully human is achieved through a simple shift in perception.

- Elevating yourself beyond the common experience of struggle and suffering is completely natural.

- Perception of perfection is your birthright and easily obtained.

CHAPTER 3

Feeling, Thinking, and Acting

"The ancestor of every action is a thought."

— RALPH WALDO EMERSON

A Peek Inside Your Mind

Which is more powerful: what you think or what you are? When you are angry, you have angry thoughts. When you are happy, you have happy thoughts. It seems that thoughts are influenced by what you feel. Even if you consider yourself a logical, unbiased thinker, you are still influenced by what you feel that day. In fact, our thoughts may change from moment to moment as our emotions change. We might be looking out our window on a cold rainy day, feeling sad and lonely because a loved one has moved to another city. Our thoughts lack energy and enthusiasm. Our emotional state is reflected in our flat, colorless thinking. Then we have a fond memory of that person. We remember a tender time when we felt close to each other, and we start to feel a little better. As a result, our thoughts begin to liven up as the bittersweet memories flicker across the screen of our mind. Next, we might see ourselves sitting over coffee in the kitchen of their new home. Our mood lightens, and correspondingly, our thoughts contain more life and movement. Finally, we decide on a whim to leave that very day to pay them a visit. Immediately we are exhilarated. Joy and excitement wash over us, and our thoughts turn lovingly toward packing, travel plans, and finally the elation of being reunited. This remarkable emotional metamorphosis from sad and lonely to joyful elation easily evolved from a few fertile spaces between the beating of our heart. The shift from lifeless, dreary thoughts to dynamic, life-supporting thoughts was made just as quickly, driven before the swelling waves of emotion. Emotions can have great impact on our thinking.

It is our common experience that emotions influence thinking. If we take it a step further, we will recognize that our thinking influences the action we perform. For instance, sadness produced low-energy thoughts, which produce low-energy action. In our previous example, the action produced from sad thinking was looking listlessly out the window. The action created when we decided to reunite with our loved one was energetic and purposeful. So, we can see that a hierarchy is being established. Emotions influence thinking, and thinking influences action. But does the realization that emotions affect thinking and action help us answer my question posed at the beginning of this chapter? Yes, in a way, but it is leading us in the wrong direction. To answer the question, "Which is more powerful: what you think or what you are?" we need to move deeper into the subtle reaches of our mind, away from the disruptive activity of thinking and action. We need to discover what influences our emotions; what makes us feel the way we feel.

Take a minute to ponder these questions. What are you feeling right now? Why are you feeling that emotion? Is it the weather, the food you ate, your job, your friends, your belief in a better world? All of these elements can dictate how we feel from time to time, but they are relative influences, aren't they? How we react to the weather or criticism from a friend depends on something much deeper within us, something that is so subtle and all-permeating that we are rarely aware that it even exists. That part of us that holds sway over our emotions, and necessarily over our thinking and action, is ultimately responsible for how successful we are in life. This powerful part of us is our inner security.

So, our hierarchy is shaping up to look like this:

security → emotion → thinking → action

At the risk of oversimplifying the subject, I will say that the concept of inner security is pretty uncomplicated. Either you are secure or you are not. (How secure we are is measured by our self-esteem. If we have high self-esteem, we are secure; if our self-esteem is low, the opposite is true. I prefer to use security, however, because the word *self-esteem* usually carries with it a negative charge or detrimental connotation.) When you are secure, it is evidenced by an inner confidence, peace, and stability. Insecurity breeds anxiety, doubt, and distrust. We are usually unaware of our level of security, as it inhabits a distant and soundless place in our mind. Because the seat of security is so indistinct, we focus on its more tangible expressions like emotions, thinking, and actions. Whether we are aware of how secure we are or not it still holds sway over every thought, word, and action we perform.

Here is an excerpt from another book of mine, *Beyond Happiness,* which perfectly illustrates this point.

Let's suppose that you have worked for a company for 18 years. Like many companies, it is experiencing a host of problems and one of the corrective measures it has enlisted is downsizing. In your office, several people have already been let go, some of them senior to you. There are strong rumors that your whole department will be eliminated.

You have been an exemplary employee. You have been loyal, energetic, and only missed work 17 times in 18 years. You are a team player and have saved the company thousands of dollars during your tenure by helping to streamline office procedures.

It is Friday afternoon, the chosen time of execution. When you returned from lunch, there on your desk was a pink office memo asking you to immediately report to your boss' office. Your mind is a whirlwind of thoughts and emotions, all malicious. You are feeling betrayed. You are angry, defensive, and afraid.

You are swept away by a flood of thoughts, which go something like this. *I've given this company the best years of my life. They never appreciated me or my work or me. Sure my boss has been nice but I never trusted him. And what's with that squirrelly growth on his upper lip he calls a mustache? He probably drinks too much and kicks the dog. God, I hate this company.*

On the way to the boss' office, you start to notice that your stomach is tied in knots, your palms are sweating, and your legs are weak. These are physical symptoms brought on by agitated thoughts bubbling in a stew of volcanic emotions.

When you walk into the office, there sits your boss behind his expensive desk with several golf clubs leaning against the wall. He begins to speak, "As you know the company has been cutting back in all departments. Soon your department will be completely eliminated."

"I knew it," you hiss under your breath. "My world is over."

He continues, "You are one of our most valued employees. You have been a great asset and your loyalty has been noted and greatly appreciated. A new department is being formed to help our company make this transition, and we would like you to manage it for us. While your hours will remain the same, we would like to offer you a significant rise in salary. What do you say?"

In an instant, you are transformed. You now love your company. You love your job, and you even love your boss' squirrelly mustache. You are convinced that he is a saint, and his dog is lucky to have him. All of your unpleasant bodily symptoms have been replaced by the physical equivalent of joy. You are on top of the world.

This is an excellent depiction of how inner security is based on perception. If we perceive danger or discord, we feel insecure. If we perceive harmony and support, we settle comfortably into our setting. But what is it that we perceive that makes us feel insecure? Or more important, what insight allows us to be at home within a world of chaos, war, and wanton waste of natural and human resources? What is this harmonizing medium within us, and how do we access it? The answer to that, my friend, is more simple than you can imagine.

Main Points for Chapter 3

- It is our common experience that emotions influence thinking, and thinking influences our actions.

- The level of our security determines the kind of emotions we have.

- Increased security is evidenced by an inner confidence, peace, and stability. Insecurity breeds anxiety, doubt, and mistrust.

- We are usually unaware of our level of security, as it inhabits a distant and soundless place deep within our mind.

- It is our perception of how secure we are that determines the quality of our emotions, thinking, and actions.

CHAPTER 4

Finding Security

"I'm astounded by people who want to know the universe when it's hard enough to find your way around Chinatown."

— WOODY ALLEN

The Cart Before the Horse

Our minds are capable of producing many great thoughts and theories, both helpful and destructive. Emotional needs are the spur for great inventions on the material plane outside the mind. The compassion for starving children mobilizes our minds to create rescue organizations that coordinate efforts worldwide. Anger and mistrust spawn unbelievable weapons that hold enormous destructive influence. Yes, our minds exhibit remarkable organizing power. The unfortunate thing is that power is often out of control. But there is something that surpasses our mind in both power and harmony. It is beyond the reach of our mind and yet completely fills it. It is the progenitor and protector of every mind in creation, including yours. It is pure awareness.

I have spoken at length in previous books about pure awareness and so will not dwell on it to any great degree here. It is only important to know that it exists and that awareness of pure awareness is vital to the full and harmonious functioning of not only your thoughts and emotions but the health of your body and the quality of its actions. Awareness of pure awareness is also responsible for how you perceive your place in your immediate environment, the world, and, in fact, the entire universe.

Shortly you will learn to effortlessly become aware of pure awareness, and from that platform of harmony, peace, and infinite potential, you will know how to quiet destructive emotions, organize thinking, and create powerful action that will bring you success in a way that is so natural, easy, and fun you will wonder why everyone isn't already doing it. Actually, I have been wondering that very same thing for years. Humans, that means you and me, are meant to be free and fun loving. We have all the equipment it takes, but it seems we're looking down the barrel of the gun rather than through the sights. We've got our lives turned around by placing value on the fruits of our labor and little on the organizing influence behind it. Well, that is about to change. Are you ready? Good, let's get to it.

Experience: Finding Nothing

Turn your head all the way to your left and look at an object.

Now quickly turn your head all the way to your right and look at another object.

What was in your mind while your head was turning from the first object to the second object? Nothing, right? Your mind was completely blank. Do it again and again if you like. The result will always be the same . . . nothing!

What is that nothing? "Well Frank," you say, "that seems a bit of a strange question. Nothing is nothing." But it turns out that this *nothing* is not empty. There is something in it: something that your mind missed, something that is the essence of not only all that we survey but all that we are. What on earth could I possibly be talking about? Let's find out.

Watching the Movie of You

Do the Finding Nothing exercise again. Look at an object on your left and then quickly turn your head to the right to find a second object. The mind was blank in between, but you were still aware, were you not? You didn't decide to take a trip down memory lane or mentally make out your last will and testament, did you? While your mind was empty of thoughts, you were still aware, right? Because your mind was between objects as your head turned, your mind turned off, leaving the screen of pure awareness with nothing projected on it. Thinking wasn't needed, so you were left alone with just uncluttered awareness to keep you company. That is what I call pure awareness, because you are not conscious of some thought, emotion, or form. You are aware of pure awareness. In fact, you are pure awareness. Pure awareness is your basic nature. Everything you know and experience is founded on pure awareness. Buddha put it this way: "To see nothing is to perceive the Way." The Beatles said, "Nothing's gonna change my world." And Frank says, "There's nothing to it." What do we mean?

When you become aware of a tree, the impression it makes in your mind is projected onto the screen of pure awareness. That is what we call a thought. In this case, it is a thought about the tree. It is not the tree itself, right? This thought of the tree is imprinted on pure awareness, like a movie is imprinted on the screen at the front of the theater. The screen was always there, and the movie didn't start until the images were projected on the screen. It is the same with your mind. Living doesn't start until the images of life, the thoughts, emotions, and perceptions from the outside world are projected on the screen of your mind, pure awareness.

The problem comes when we forget pure awareness and believe that the images projected in our mind are real. We think that the tree in our mind is an accurate representation of the real tree in our backyard. That would be like going to a movie and believing you are a character in the movie being projected on the screen. When you believe you are part of the movie, you weep and laugh, fall in and out of love, and experience all the drama the movie has to offer. Behind it all, supporting all the images of the movie, is the screen. Without it there would be no movie. As a moviegoer, you already know this. But as a person living in your mind, you have forgotten that all the images of your life could not exist if they were not reflected on pure awareness: the screen of your mind.

When you become aware of pure awareness, something most remarkable happens. You become free from the burdens that have defined your life until now. You enjoy an effortlessness, a fitting into the flow of life. You don't feel like you are swimming upstream or the flow of life is passing you by while you are caught helplessly in an eddy along the bank. Not to mix metaphors, but you take yourself out of the drama of the movie and take a seat in the audience. There you can enjoy completely the best of both worlds. In the audience, you enjoy the security of being beyond the belief that what you are seeing is real. You can enjoy the movie for what it is: an allusion of life. You see? Perception of pure awareness is the missing piece in the security, emotion, thinking, action hierarchy.

When you are aware of pure awareness, you are aware of your basic nature, which is unbounded and unchanging. Your basic nature: pure awareness is your true essence beyond suffering and death. So, in light of what we have just learned, the answer to the question, "Which is more powerful, what you think or what you are?" is obviously *what you are*. (And you thought I forgot all about that question, didn't you?)

When you are aware of pure awareness, you are secure. When you become aware of pure awareness, you are a cosmic sponge soaking up the expansive stability, the strength, peace, and joy of pure awareness. Soon and without effort, emotional and mental discord begin to melt into the vastness of your Self. You draw from the peace and harmony and absolute stability that pure awareness is, and your life becomes a reflection of those qualities. When you are not aware of pure awareness . . . well, you already know how that feels.

Aware of pure awareness → unwavering security →
healthy emotion → clear thinking → dynamic action

Becoming aware of pure awareness is a great adventure, but there is more. And now we come to the focus of this book: Eufeeling (short for "euphoric feeling") and what it will bring to your life. Simply put, Eufeeling will fulfill your deepest desire. That's right, the deepest, most desperate desire, hiding in the deepest, most desolate part of your mind will be fulfilled when you come to know Eufeeling. Not bad for starters, wouldn't you say? But here's the really neat thing. Anyone can easily experience Eufeeling, and that means you. You don't have to take my word for it, for shortly you will prove it to yourself.

Not to get too far ahead of myself, but I'm excited to share this with you, after you and Eufeeling become old buddies, I have another surprise for you. I want you to learn how to rewrite the movie that is your life. After Eufeeling is established in your awareness, you will learn how to begin to get the things you want from life: more money, deeper relationships, a more fulfilling job, travel, more free time, and very important, more fun. But before we change your world from the inside out, let's take a few minutes to learn about Eufeeling and how it works the wonders it performs.

Main Points for Chapter 4

- Pure awareness is beyond the reach of your mind and yet completely fills it.

- We've got our lives turned around by placing value on the fruits of our labor rather than on the source of their existence.

- The nothing between thoughts is pure awareness.

- Pure awareness is your basic nature. Everything you know and experience is founded on pure awareness.

- Living doesn't start until the images of life are projected on the screen of your mind: pure awareness.

- Perception of pure awareness is the missing piece in the security, emotion, thinking, action hierarchy.

- When you are aware of pure awareness, you are completely secure.

Chapter 5

Eufeeling

"And in the end, it's not the years in your life that count. It's the life in your years."

— Abraham Lincoln

Your Mind Loves Eufeeling

Eufeeling is a most remarkable entity. It is unique in creation as it is both unbounded and finite. It is the first glimmering of consciousness in our mind, the first rays of creative light on their way to becoming the things and thoughts of our world. Eufeeling is the only *thing* that is free of contradiction and restriction.

Your mind loves Eufeeling. It is at once the essence of your inner being and the promise of joys yet unrealized. Settled in the awareness of Eufeeling, your mind wants for nothing. Eufeeling is completely safe, and when you are aware of Eufeeling, you are safe. It is the foundation for the unshakable security we all seek. The Eufeeling mind navigates the treacherous jungles of this perilous world with perfect precision, so you can revel in its beauty, untouched by its thorns.

The prefix *eu* comes from the Greek meaning well, good, or true. I like to think of Eufeeling as *true* feeling. For something to be true, it should maintain itself, stand in its own truth, so to speak. It shouldn't break apart, dissolve, or transform into something different. It should remain stable and unchangeable. Every created thing has a birth, a life, and finally dissolves or dies. That is why I call life the field of death. Everything must die; everything, that is, except Eufeeling. The ultimate truth should not change. Pure awareness is ultimate and unchanging. It is unborn and undying. Eufeeling is the only created thing that shares that attribute with pure awareness. It is always there, always ready to support and guide.

Eufeeling has always been and always will be. It does not come and go like the relative emotions that burst like fireworks in the darkness of our mind. It is the soft, pure light of dawn. Eufeeling is with you right now. Can you feel it? It has been with you all through your life, waiting for you to recognize it. And you have recognized it from time to time, when life was at its richest. Eufeeling may have unexpectedly stolen over you while sitting serenely on a park bench or by the bank of a quietly whispering brook. You have felt its deep delight in a lover's tender touch or been completely consumed by its bliss in the throes of all-out passion.

Eufeeling is ever watchful. It is waiting for just the slightest indication that you want it in your life. It is ever ready, with arms open, welcoming you like a mother whose child has been too long away. You could say that Eufeeling is an open door waiting for you to walk through.

Your mind identifies Eufeeling as joy, peace, stillness, silence, unbounded love, bliss, ecstasy, and so forth. Eufeelings are not feelings. Feelings like happiness, excitement, anger, grief, conditional love, jealousy, fear, and so on come and go with the conditions of life. They are subservient to conditions like getting money, losing money, losing a loved one, or getting a new job. Feelings continually control your mind with the color of that emotion. Eufeeling is the purity beyond your mind, the canvas on which your emotions are painted.

There is actually only one Eufeeling. When Eufeeling first begins to take form at the finest level of creation, it reflects the oneness of pure awareness. The mind cannot perceive oneness, so it cannot perceive the oneness of Eufeeling at this level. But soon, Eufeeling begins to warm up to the business of creation. As it begins to congeal, it draws around it more form. These first forms deep within the mind are the reflections of the purity of Eufeeling. These reflections of Eufeeling are like the colors of the rainbow that fracture from a single ray of pure sunlight. You recognize these rainbow colors of Eufeeling as peace and love and bliss. So, it seems to the mind that there are many Eufeelings, but in reality, there is only unbounded stillness.

When relative emotions are reflected in your mind, they always have to do with concerns about the past or the future. Think about it. If you are worried or anxious about something, your mind is captivated in the future. When you're feeling guilt, remorse, or grief, your mind is lodged in the past. Conditional feelings come in all shapes and sizes and intensities. We rarely have pure emotions. So, what we normally get is a passionate mixture: some stronger, some weaker. What we end up with is a kind of emotional stew, bubbling and boiling just below our level of conscious awareness, but having a marked effect on our outward behavior just the same. This is way too complicated for our concern. We will leave the tasting of that emotional stew to psychological professionals and related fields. Eufeeling is free of the influence of cause and effect. It is simple, pure, and singular, and that is where our story begins.

The Snake That Swallows Its Tail

I have worked hard all of my adult life. I worked especially hard at becoming enlightened. To me, enlightenment was a state of eternal happiness. In my mind, I had this utopian idea that when I was enlightened, I would walk on a cloud of bliss, looking down on the suffering masses and saying to myself, *Tsk, tsk. Look at all those suffering people down there. I sure am glad I am above it all.*

Enlightenment became my goal, and I had a burning desire to reach that goal as quickly as possible. Little did I know the very desire that put me on the path to freedom actually imprisoned me in a never-ending labyrinth that continually turned back on itself. Desire is Ouroboros: the snake that swallows its own tail. When desire is done with you, there is nothing left, which, if you can accept it, is a good thing. Nothing is the beginning and the end of the path. It also happens to be the middle as well, but few recognize it as so.

Here's a tip. Whenever you are on a path to find unbounded bliss and eternal freedom, get off that path immediately. If something is unbounded and eternal, it must already be where you are. So, you don't need a path to get you where you already are, because you are already there. Does that make sense? Stop making an effort, and peace will be waiting for you, like stillness after a violent storm.

Experience: Finding Nothing on the Path

Begin to perform a simple action, like putting down the book you are reading or walking across the room. Any simple activity will do. Somewhere during the act, suddenly stop moving. Immediately when you stop, pay attention to what is in your mind. Then pay attention to what your body is feeling.

When you stop in the middle of any action, you will find your mind empty and your body still. No matter where you are or what you are doing, be it a single action or your life's journey, *nothing* is always there with you . . . always!

You need a path for relative things like finding the grocery store and achieving financial security. Paths are necessary to reach out for and find the relative things in our lives. But when it comes to securing something that is everywhere all the time, like pure awareness and Eufeeling, a path is pretty much useless. Actually, it is worse than useless. It is a waste of life.

You can't get something you already have no matter how hard you try. If you believe there is a path to unbounded love, your belief is blinding you. You can't see the forest for the trees. You can try and try and try, creating great effort for many years, and you will still not be able to get what you already have. How do I know? Because I already tried and tried and tried.

One time I quit trying and felt so good that I thought, *If not trying makes me feel so good, imagine how much peace I can get if I really worked it.* Do you see the lunacy in this thinking? Peace comes from less activity, not more. Our peaceful moments don't come while we're multitasking. They come when our mind is at rest. If I'd stayed in the *stop trying* mode, peace would have been permanent. Instead, I tried and tried and tried some more.

This is a common mistake. Once we reach a goal, once we get something we've worked hard for, we feel pretty good. We think we feel good because we got what we wanted. In reality, the deeper, inner good feeling comes because we don't have to try to get that thing anymore. There is a little space of complete non-doing, and it is filled with joy or peace or a sense of satisfaction. Because we misunderstand the nature of peace, we try to fill that space with more activity. Soon after we reach a goal, we start to feel antsy and immediately turn to find another mountain to climb.

Sometimes we can't even enjoy our moment of stillness, because our mind is already looking ahead to the next conquest. It knows that happiness is fleeting. The mind is ever searching for that permanent happiness. This is where Eufeeling comes in.

Eufeeling is everywhere all the time. That's why I said that it has always been with you. If Eufeeling is there with you right now and you are not aware of it, where should you go, and what should you do to find it? The incredibly simple answer is that there is nowhere to go and nothing to do except become aware of it. And how should you become aware of it? The answer is, without trying and creating effort. This is the secret, the key to unlocking the amulet of suffering you have been carrying around your neck since you left your childhood behind. Stop trying.

Here's an exercise to demonstrate what I mean.

Experience: How to Perceive Without Effort

Think of a number from one to ten. Now, picture a color in your mind. Finally, think of a tall tree. Now one right after the other, think of the number, the color, and the tree.

When you thought of the number and then thought of the color, how hard was it for your mind to go from one to the other? Did you say, *Okay mind, let's think of the number. And now that we have the number in mind, let's work our way over to think about the color. Now we have the color firmly in mind, let's go over and think about the tree.* Of course, your mind doesn't work this way at all. It moved automatically and without effort from one object to the other. The whole process was effortless.

Now this exercise is a little misleading, because it doesn't teach you how to perceive without effort. You already do that. The real value of this exercise is to make you consciously aware of how effortless the process of perceiving is. Any trying on your part would only get in the way.

So, what have we learned so far? For starters, Eufeeling is unbounded, and because it is everywhere, all the time, it has always been with you. Regular emotions like anger and anxiety are not unbounded. They are bound to our past and our future, to our memories and our hopes and fears. The flavor and intensity of our emotions depend on how secure we feel at any given moment. We can be tossed about by the waves of emotions, like a rudderless ship on a stormy ocean. Or we can anchor to the stability of Eufeeling, resulting in inner peace, joy, and love. We don't have to do anything to become aware of Eufeeling except to perceive it. Perceiving is effortless, therefore, perceiving Eufeeling is effortless.

So, you might ask, "If perceiving Eufeeling is so effortless, how come I have not been able to perceive it?" Yes, perceiving is effortless, but it is like the beam of a flashlight. You just point the beam at what you want to observe, and, presto changeo, you see the illuminated object glowing in your awareness. But no matter how effortless the process is, if you point the flashlight in the wrong direction, you will never find what you are looking for. The only reason Eufeeling eludes you is because you are looking in the wrong direction. Once you learn how to find Eufeeling—that is, the direction you must turn in order to perceive it—you will never lose it again. It is my job to turn you in the right direction and then step out of the way while you and Eufeeling get to know each other.

Main Points for Chapter 5

- Every created thing, except Eufeeling, has a birth, a life, and finally dissolves or dies.

- Eufeeling is unique in creation as it is both unbounded and finite.

- Eufeeling is with you right now.

- Eufeeling is not a relative feeling like anger, grief, or happiness, but your mind identifies

Eufeeling as joy, peace, stillness, silence, unbounded love, bliss, ecstasy, and so on.

- Relative emotions always have to do with our past or future. Eufeeling is awareness of present perfection.

- Eufeeling is right here, right now. You don't need a path to get to where you already are.

- Inner peace (Eufeeling) comes when you stop trying.

- To find Eufeeling, there is nowhere to go and nothing to do except *become aware of it.*

CHAPTER 6

How Quantum Entrainment Works

"Do you wish to be great? Then begin by being. Do you desire to construct a vast and lofty fabric? Think first about the foundations of humility. The higher your structure is to be, the deeper must be its foundation."

— SAINT AUGUSTINE

Offering Your Mind a Banana

The minds of most people, most of the time, are on autopilot. That is, thinking is taking place, but the thinker is pretty much unaware of what is going on. Their thoughts lazily serpentine through the mental mush that fills most of the waking hours of each day. Except for the occasional times when it is needed, like slamming on the brake when it sees the sudden red flare of brake lights ahead or when it receives any imposing a letter from the IRS, the common observer is not really paying attention. It's like turning on the radio and forgetting about it. Most of the day, it is just background noise until a familiar song is played and awareness *wakes up* to listen to a few bars before slipping back into the more ordinary, everyday, distracted consciousness. This unaware thinking I call common consciousness. It is weak, undisciplined, and destructive. Common consciousness is the symptom of thinking without opening to the embrace of Eufeeling.

QE is the process that connects common consciousness with Eufeeling. QE awakens the unmanageable mind to the joy of orderly awareness. It takes your awareness from the chaotic turbulence of common consciousness to the absolute perfect order of pure awareness beyond your mind. There are no thoughts in pure awareness. Pure awareness is not pure energy: it is beyond energy. Pure awareness is not perfect order: it is beyond order. So, you can see that pure awareness is *nothing,* and if you were hanging out in pure awareness all day long, you would get *nothing* done, literally. (So there is hope for those of you who have had a friend or family member tell you that you will amount to nothing.)

Common consciousness creates chaos and suffering. Pure awareness doesn't create anything. If we are sidetracked by auto-thinking common consciousness, we are not aware of pure awareness. If we are aware of pure awareness, we are aware of nothing else. So, what are we to do? Neither state alone affords us the joy of being fully human. I would like to emphasize the word *fully* here. Living in one state or the other is incomplete. The answer is to combine the active common consciousness with unbounded pure awareness. When QE entices your mind to go beyond itself in pure awareness, it doesn't ask you to stay there. Neither does it allow you to return to the destructive tendencies of unfounded thinking. QE is quite clever. It offers your mind what it has been looking for all along: Eufeeling. Eufeeling anchors your mind to unbounded pure awareness while at the same time allowing it to be actively thinking, feeling, and creating perfect harmony in its infinite expressions.

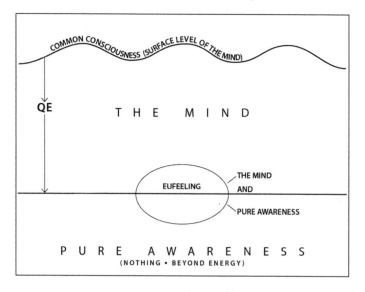

This is not something you must train your mind to do. In fact, if you have ever tried to train your mind to do anything, much less nothing, you know how much effort and energy you must bring to the task. Becoming aware of Eufeeling is something the mind is yearning to do and does so gladly once it is given the chance. Like offering a banana to a monkey, QE offers the mind something most delicious and *a peeling*. (Pun intended to wake up those of you who might have just slipped back into common consciousness.) For the mischievous mind, Eufeeling is that banana. Easily and without effort, common consciousness becomes settled in the sweet security of all-embracing Eufeeling.

This state of expanded awareness, when your mind is receptive to Eufeeling, is called QE Awareness. Fully engaged in QE Awareness, your mind cannot be agitated, distracted, revengeful, lustful, contrary, or confused. When your mind is absorbed in beauty or love or joy, it is sensitive to Eufeeling in QE Awareness. Think about the times of greatest joy and love in your life. Could you at those times be anxious, angry, or distracted? Impossible! When Eufeeling is reflected in your mind, you are incapable of discord or dissonance. At these times, you stand firmly on the foundation of what it is to be fully human. From this foundation of QE Awareness, you are capable of creating only the greatest good. You have stepped into that country inhabited by the greatest sages, artists, teachers, humanists, and healers in our world. We will talk more about what it means to be a fully human being after you have learned how easy it is to become one.

All this talk about Eufeeling has whet my appetite for the actual experience of Eufeeling. How about you? Are you ready to leave common consciousness behind in favor of thinking and feeling from the purity and peace of Eufeeling? Well, I've always felt it bad form to keep someone waiting. So, without fanfare or further ado, it is now time for me to introduce you to Eufeeling.

Main Points for Chapter 6

- Common consciousness is the symptom of thinking without opening to the embrace of Eufeeling.

- Neither common consciousness nor pure awareness alone affords us the joy of being fully human.

- QE is the process that connects common consciousness with Eufeeling.

- Becoming aware of Eufeeling is something the mind is yearning to do and does so gladly once it is given the chance.

- QE Awareness is when you are aware of Eufeeling while you are performing daily activity.

- From this foundation of QE Awareness, you are capable of creating only the greatest good.

- Once you enter QE Awareness you step into that country inhabited by the greatest sages, artists, teachers, humanists, and healers in our world.

CHAPTER 7

How to Do
Quantum Entrainment
(How to Know Eufeeling)

"Enlightenment is the understanding that this is all,
that this is perfect, that this is it. Enlightenment is not
an achievement, it is an understanding that there is
nothing to achieve, nowhere to go."

— Osho

Mental Pole Vaulting

You may have heard of Quantum Entrainment or QE.
Quantum Entrainment is the formal name I have given
to the process of perceiving Eufeeling. QE leads common
consciousness into pure awareness, and there it perceives
Eufeeling. So, QE is successful when it stops working. It
invites the common conscious mind to naturally drop

into the nonactive state of pure awareness. At that point, its job is over. If we continued to *do* something to *stay* in pure awareness, the activity of doing would expel us from that state of perfect stillness. QE is like the pole a pole-vaulter uses to lift him over the high bar. Once he has reached his zenith, he lets go of the pole. Holding onto the pole would knock down the high bar and undo everything he had worked for. After years of training, in the end, the pole-vaulter is only successful when he lets go of everything. Only when he is suspended in midair over the bar, free of all effort and training, is he successful. So is it with your mind. Only when it lets go of training and effort can it be completely still. The beauty of the QE process is that it gets out of the way and lets your mind rest peacefully in QE Awareness.

QE is a process that leads to non-doing. How could non-doing be anything but easy? You can't work hard to do nothing. It is self-defeating, isn't it? Doing QE is simple and easy, and learning QE is, too. QE is simple, but it is precise, so make sure you follow the directions completely. Very soon now, you will walk through your world awake in QE Awareness.

(*Please note:* Some of you may like to learn the QE Triangulation healing technique as a preparation for the more refined QE process that follows. It is good practice and will help you become more familiar with the subtle reflections of Eufeeling in your mind. QE Triangulation is a simple, three-step, mechanical process that quickly and easily leads common consciousness into pure awareness and Eufeeling. It is the basic QE healing technique that hundreds of thousands of people have learned just by reading these instructions. It is best done with a partner but can be done on yourself if no partner is available.

To learn the QE Triangulation healing technique, turn to the Appendix. The chapter "How to Heal in Three Steps" from my first book, *The Secret of Instant Healing,* is printed in its entirety.)

Learning QE

In preparation for learning QE, find yourself a quiet place with a comfortable chair where you won't be disturbed by family, friends, pets, or phones for a full 30 minutes. You can also have somebody read these instructions to you, as long as they only read what is written and do not engage you in conversation. Or you can record the instructions, making sure to leave blank space when instructions call for time with eyes closed. Okay, ready?

Sit comfortably and close your eyes. Just let your mind wander wherever it wants to go for 15 to 30 seconds. Just watch your thoughts as they come and go. Now, become more aware of what you are thinking. The content doesn't matter. Just pay very close attention to any thoughts that flow across the screen of your mind. Watch them with focused attention. That doesn't mean you should make an effort to try and watch them or concentrate on them. Be easy, with a focused attention like a cat watching a mouse hole. Continue to watch your thoughts with an easy, focused attention for one to two minutes.

Don't read any further until you have closely watched your thoughts for one or two minutes. I'll wait. . . .

Okay, have you just finished one or two minutes, attentively and easily watching your thoughts? Good, then let's continue.

As you innocently observed your thoughts, you will have noticed that they became quieter and slowed down almost immediately, isn't that right? They didn't seem as loud. They became fainter and fewer as your thinking became softer. Remember that whatever your thoughts are doing is just right. Whether your thoughts are noisy or quiet doesn't matter; your job is to be the perfect observer. You just watch to see what they'll do next. That's all you must do: observe with quiet attention.

Did you happen to notice that at times your thoughts stopped all together? As your thoughts became fainter, you may have noticed that they died away, and you were left alone with just pure awareness. Neat, huh? But we're just getting started.

Did you also notice that after you did the first part of this exercise, you felt more relaxed in the body and more quiet in the mind? These are delicious benefits of becoming aware of pure awareness, whether you were aware of it or not. Soon you will be functioning on this quiet, more refined level even in the midst of the most hectic daily episodes. But we have more to do, so let's get back to it.

Again, close your eyes. Innocently and with attention, watch your thoughts as before. This time, it will be easier, and you might find your thoughts quickly settling down or stopping altogether. Attentively observe in this way for a couple of minutes. After two or three minutes, note how you feel.

Again, I'll wait. . . .

During those two or three minutes, you will have felt some quietness, some settling down. Along with it, you will have noticed something like stillness, silence, or peace. Note that you feel better when they are there. You may also have felt joy, love, compassion, elation, or bliss. Take a moment and identify the good feeling you are having. That good feeling is your Eufeeling.

This time when you sit with your eyes closed, this is what I would like you to do . . . watch your thoughts, and wait for your Eufeeling to rise in your awareness. Remember, your Eufeeling could be something as simple as stillness or silence or as profound as ecstasy. One Eufeeling is no better than another. Whatever your Eufeeling is, just easily observe it. If thoughts return, innocently observe them. Then your thoughts will give way to either no thought (pure awareness) or Eufeeling. Whichever is there—thoughts, Eufeeling, or pure awareness—observe it with simple innocence and do nothing else. This is very important: do nothing but watch your thoughts and wait for your Eufeeling. When your Eufeeling is in your awareness, focus on it clearly and intently. When nothing is happening, you are aware of pure awareness. At that time, you simply wait in pure awareness until your Eufeeling rises again. Then enjoy the depth and flavor of Eufeeling by clearly and easily observing it.

Do you see how simple this is? Whatever appears on the screen of your mind, your position is always the same. You are the observer, nothing more. *Never interfere or try to control either your thoughts or your Eufeeling.* Believe me, everything will be taken care of for you. Did you have to work at becoming relaxed or feeling peaceful? No, it's all automatic. It's all taken care of for you through the wisdom of your Eufeeling once you become aware of it. Don't complicate it, or you will step back on the path of struggling and suffering.

Now resume the QE process with eyes closed, just as I have described it previously. Do this session for about five minutes. When you are done, take enough time to slowly open your eyes and continue reading. . . .

How are you feeling right now? Are you aware of your Eufeeling? Guess what? Your eyes are open, and you are aware of your Eufeeling. Isn't that remarkable? Before, you had to close your eyes and dive deep within your mind to find it. But look what has happened. Eufeeling has followed you out into activity. How cool is that?

Remember that Eufeeling is unbounded, so it is always there. You have just been ignoring it most of your life. And you will ignore it again. But very quickly, by doing QE regularly, you will always have it in a moment's reflection. You are building the foundation for a life that is beyond imagination. Somewhere in the not-too-distant future, you will all of a sudden realize that you are living life in bliss, beyond your greatest expectations.

Now, we are not quite done. In fact, the best is just ahead. I'd like you to continue with the QE process as you have just learned it. Close your eyes and observe what is flowing across the screen of your mind. Watch until you become aware of your Eufeeling and then observe your Eufeeling with tender attention. Not interfering, look deeply into Eufeeling. If it changes into another Eufeeling, look deeply into the new one. Do this for three to five minutes.

Then, when you feel the time is right, slowly open your eyes and continue doing QE. Sitting with eyes open, staring easily ahead of you, become aware of your

Eufeeling. Continue to do QE with eyes open. You will have thoughts, Eufeeling, and pure awareness, all with your eyes open. Continue for one or two minutes more and then slowly stand and look at some object nearby. Look at the object and then become aware of your Eufeeling. Then look at another object while observing your Eufeeling.

When you are ready, slowly walk around the room. Feel your body moving. Feel how you balance on one leg, then the other, and the pressure of the floor against each foot. When your Eufeeling is not there, just find it again through simple awareness. As you walk slowly around the room, engage all your senses. Pay attention to the noises in the room. Feel the air brush past your face. Run your hand over a plant or another object. Engage your sense of smell and taste. All the while, continue to return to your Eufeeling when you notice it is not there. Stop and become solely aware of your Eufeeling, and feel how it intensifies or changes into a different Eufeeling.

In actuality, it doesn't really change in intensity or kind. You are just becoming more aware of the infinite manifestations of your Self (Eufeeling) beyond yourself. This is *You,* the way you were meant to be. Not all tangled up in the ego-manipulated activities founded on fear but just simply being with your Self. Nothing is more important or fulfilling. Falling in love with your environment while aware of your Eufeeling is called QE Awareness. It is the foundation for fullness and unbounded appreciation for what is. We will set a little time aside for you to get used to observing your world through your new eyes. After a short time for creating balance with QE Awareness, you will learn QE Intention: how to make personal suggestions and private requests of Mother Nature.

Then, from the fullness of QE Awareness, watch as she builds your new world for you.

A Quick Review of What You Just Learned

- Sit comfortably with your eyes closed, and let your mind wander for 10 to 15 seconds.

- Watch your thoughts with simple innocence, like a cat watching a mouse hole.

- In time, your thoughts will become quieter, slower, or disappear altogether.

- Continue to quietly observe whatever happens.

- Soon you will feel some good feeling: your Eufeeling.

- Now observe your Eufeeling with clear, simple innocence.

- It will get stronger or change to another Eufeeling or thoughts will come.

- Whatever happens, just observe it unfolding, as if you were watching a movie.

- When you open your eyes, continue this simple process of innocent observation.

- Move around the room, slowly interacting with objects.

- When you realize your Eufeeling has slipped away, just look to see what you are feeling. Observe it for a while and then continue to explore other objects. This is QE Awareness.

Main Points for Chapter 7

- QE leads common consciousness into pure awareness, and there it perceives Eufeeling.

- The beauty of QE is that it gets out of the way and lets your mind rest peacefully in QE Awareness.

- During the QE process, *never interfere or try to control either your thoughts or your Eufeeling.*

- Whatever happens, just observe it unfolding, as if you were watching a movie.

- Remember that Eufeeling is unbounded, so it is always there. All you need to do is become aware of it. Becoming aware of something is effortless.

- QE Awareness, Eufeeling in activity, is *You* the way you were meant to be.

❧

CHAPTER 8

Living at the Bottom of Your Mind

"I define joy as a sustained sense of well-being and internal peace—a connection to what matters."

— OPRAH WINFREY

Beyond the Touch of Time

By uncovering Eufeeling within you, you have discovered the pivot point around which all life revolves. When you become aware of Eufeeling, your life becomes anchored in the unshakable, unbounded essence of creation beyond the touch of time. Without awareness of Eufeeling, life is unbalanced. But this is no longer your concern, at least personally. Now that you are among the newly awakened, there is no time to sit around on your laurels. Yes, the perception of Eufeeling is effortless, but unless you plan to live in a cave, you must take a little time to integrate Eufeeling into your daily activity.

I've written two books, *The Secret of Instant Healing* and *The Secret of Quantum Living,* that will give you step-by-step instruction on how to create mini-miracles daily and, from time to time, some pretty big ones. You'll learn to heal physical pains and problems along with mental disharmony. You will also learn to apply QE for everything from athletics to eating and sleeping. In *The Secret of Quantum Living,* there is a whole chapter devoted to teaching QE to our children, the parchment upon which our future will be written. I suggest you refer to these works for more detailed applications of Eufeeling in your life. You will be amazed, delighted, and titillated as you discover how to apply your newfound awareness to everyday situations.

Our focus in this book, however, will take us in a different, less-obvious direction. When you learned QE, you learned to go beyond mental and emotional activity into pure awareness. Then, instead of forgetting about pure awareness and returning to the relative world, you learned to perceive Eufeeling. Eufeeling anchors your awareness at the deepest, most silent level of your mind, where thoughts are created. Sitting, settled in the bliss of Eufeeling, you actually become a witness to creation. As soon as you are comfortable with your role as witness, you will learn how to create from that most subtle and powerful level of life deep within the mind. This process of creating power and grace in your life, not to mention wealth and wellness, is called QE Intention. Once you learn QE Intention, you will become the master of creation, and you won't have to do a thing.

You will learn non-doing and, from there, be able to satisfy your desires. You will set in motion subtle, potent forces that will form around those desires to manifest them on the material plane. You will learn how to use QE Intention for financial freedom, emotional management, problem solving, chronic health issues and, very importantly, how to help others realize their heart's desires.

I am a great fan of simplifying things. Everywhere I look, I see people working harder and getting less done. The increased quantity and diminished quality of work seems to be directly proportional to the amount of multitasking one can do. There is a movement afoot in business to do less and get more done. Oddly enough, I see them working very hard to accomplish this. It is the nature of the unanchored mind, the active mind of modern living, to do more and more, looking for the ultimate solution. Paradoxically, it is the still mind, anchored in the deep harmony of inner peace, that has found a solution. The mantra of the QE mind is, "Do nothing, and achieve everything." Once you become comfortable hanging out at the bottom of your mind, you will learn QE Intention and how to get everything by doing nothing.

One really can't "use" Eufeeling. But you can become aware of Eufeeling in various situations and watch how it enriches the quality of life for you and those around you. It really is a most amazing process. At first, your mind will want to roll up its sleeves and get to work on the business of creation. Ego can be heard to say, "I can do great things and even manifest lots of cool material stuff in my life." This motivation is driven by the need to show some value and create some effect in one's world. That is just the ego wanting to strut its stuff. But very quickly, ego will see the sense of letting go, letting nature, or in this case, Eufeeling, take its course. It will quickly become crystal clear that creation has gotten along perfectly well until now without any help from your ego. Soon, the burden of, "I am the creator," falls gently from our shoulders, like a worn-out garment, to be replaced by the realization, "I am the observer through which creation unfolds."

Planting the Seed of the Thousand-Petaled Lotus

So, I am not going to emphasize the outward stroke of creation as I have in previous works. Instead, you will learn to settle into the profound silence of Self and from that exalted seat secretly conceal a seed whose blossom will be the thousand-petaled lotus of your life. Then inner fulfillment will be reflected in every aspect of your life. And you can also manifest lots of cool material stuff, too! So, let's move along to the next step of creating inner peace and outer abundance. You can begin by becoming aware of Eufeeling while doing quieter, less-hectic activities. Let's have you start by sitting in a chair and performing the next exercise.

Experience: Sitting with Eufeeling

Find a comfortable chair where you won't be bothered for at least 15 minutes. Turn off the phone, usher the pets from the room, close the door, and settle comfortably into your chair. Repeat "How to Do Quantum Entrainment," the exercise you learned earlier. After you have walked around the room quietly identifying Eufeeling in the objects around you, return to your seat and close your eyes. Now do the

QE process once again and become aware of Eufeeling. Do this for five minutes.

After five minutes or so, slowly move one of your fingers and then immediately become aware of Eufeeling for five to ten seconds. Next, move your whole hand and then return to Eufeeling for another five to ten seconds. Repeat this process with other parts of your body, remembering to move that part of the body and then return to Eufeeling. For example, you could go from your hand to your nose to your left eye to your right knee and then to the hair on your head. Where you go or in what order is not important. Just remember to physically move that area and then become aware of Eufeeling for five to ten seconds afterward. Now, finish off with another three to five minutes of QE, the innocent awareness of Eufeeling.

I would like to see you do the Sitting with Eufeeling exercise two to four times daily. Ideally, they would be 15-minute sessions each. But they don't have to be. If you do three or four sessions of five minutes each, that will be just fine. Do what you can, but be diligent about doing this practice every day for the next three or four days. It is important that you establish a very solid foundation of QE Awareness on which to build QE Intention. Review the instructions on how to do QE at least once a day to make sure you do not pick up any bad habits. You want to take every opportunity to spend time with Eufeeling at the bottom of your mind. It is from this level of awareness that you will create your life anew.

You don't have to restrict yourself to just sitting. Any time you think of it—driving your car, talking with a coworker, brushing your teeth, or any other activity—become aware of Eufeeling and the deep still-ness that accompanies it. Allow this to be an enjoyable activity, not a chore. You will quickly find your mind automatically going to Eufeeling when the opportunity presents itself. Just go with the flow, reminding yourself to check in with Eufeeling whenever you think of it. You may be aware of it for a few minutes or a few seconds; it doesn't matter at this point. We have a saying: "If it isn't easy and it isn't fun, it isn't QE."

For the next few days, while becoming more in tune with the peaceful, unbounded nature of Eufeeling and confirming the quiet command of QE Awareness in your daily routine, I have a few more things I would like to discuss with you. I would especially like to take a closer look at the mind, ego, desire, and the mechanics of suf-fering. I think you will find it fascinating dialogue, and I'm anxious to tell you all about it. So, hold on to your hats. We are off and running.

Main Points for Chapter 8

- The mind *unaware* of Eufeeling creates more and more activity looking for solutions to more and more problems.

- It is ego that wants to be the doer.

- The ultimate answer to the myriad problems that face us is, "Do nothing and achieve everything."

- Inner peace and outer abundance starts and ends with QE Awareness.

- Practice "Sitting with Eufeeling" several times a day, from 5 to 15 minutes each session.

- Practice QE Awareness (Eufeeling in activity) anytime you think about it during the day: driving, talking, eating, and so on.

❧

CHAPTER 9

Eufeeling, Ego, and Belief

"Nothing endures but change."

— HERACLEITUS

The Boundless Heart of Creation

Eufeeling is unbounded. It is also the first and finest expression of form. Eufeeling is like a combination of the lens and the film of a movie projector. The pure light of pure awareness shines through the Eufeeling lens and is changed into the familiar patterns of light and dark we recognize on the screen as a movie. The light and shadow on the screen is a portrayal of the life we live outside of the movie. The point I want to make here is that all created forms emanate from Eufeeling, emanate from your vital essence, from you! I guess we could more accurately call it *You*-feeling. Are you beginning to get an idea of your true status? Are you beginning to realize the role you play in the creation of this universe? You are the boundless heart of creation from which the cosmos is born, maintained, and into which it dissolves. You are not in the universe. It is in you. It is only the belief that you are the movie that prevents you from appreciating your true Self and the position you hold in the play and display eternity.

You may have heard that "You are the creator of your world." This precept is almost always misunderstood. There is a little *you* and a big *You*. The big You is Eufeeling, and the little *you* is ego. To eliminate confusion about which you I am talking about, I will refer to *You* as Self or Eufeeling and you as *me* or ego. When we are taught that we are the creator of our world, we almost always see it through the limited, cause and effect eyes of ego. This can often cause problems, as the needs of ego are limited to the individual's needs. The individual's awareness reflects the individual's needs, and the individual's needs are limited to protecting and promoting the individual. This is true by definition. Individual awareness is disconnected from universal awareness.

Even when the individual has altruistic aspirations, it is always to satisfy limited individual concerns. You may know people who take great pride in the work they do for charities, churches, the homeless, and so on. Many times these individuals will have an air of self-importance about them. In extreme cases, they become arrogant and overbearing. The other end of the spectrum finds people who are over-accommodating, almost smothering their charges with a feigned sense of service, humility, and concern. The good work they do is many times overshadowed by their forced behavior. Their performance is an outward manifestation of an ego that is unsuccessfully trying to satisfy an inner need for recognition, acceptance, or the like. The basic motivation here is no different from the person who strives for power, fame, or fortune. The only differ is the expression. It was Christ who warned us that we cannot acquire the kingdom of heaven through good deeds. Good deeds can be motivated by weakness, fear, and all manner of hidden agendas.

Ego Is a Shadow

When individual awareness expands to universal awareness, individual action is guided by universal wisdom. Universal wisdom knows what needs to be done, where it needs to be done, and when. When pure awareness shines through the lens of ego, it becomes distorted by the fears and hopes that ego carries deep within it. These distortions create cravings and lopsided desires that lead us down countless twisted and tormented roads that end only when the traveler sighs his or her last breath.

Ego is not an entity. It has no real substance. Ego is a shadow, a distortion of light and dark projected on the screen of consciousness. The symptoms of ego are the attributes that belong to me: who you are, what you want, and your reaction to what other people think of you. Ego is alive and well when you take authorship for your life. When you believe that you are your body-mind, that you are a father or a daughter, that you have a job and a family, and a future and a past, you anchor your belief to the phenomenal world of change. When you believe that any part of creation is part of your primal Self, you embrace change, and change is death.

Do you know where ego comes from? Do you know how it forms and why? Do you know how to satisfy its insatiable thirst for power? Ego can be the schoolyard bully or its fearful victim. It can be harmful or helpful, but it always acts on its own behalf. And it always acts out of fear, even when it takes on the persona of the schoolyard bully.

Ego is a piece of wholeness, or at least that is how it perceives itself. It is a sliver of shadow, darkness looking into darkness, trying to find the light. Ego is the turning of awareness away from the inner light of Self. It believes that things and thoughts can fill the empty darkness it has become. Let's take a closer look at how ego is born.

Common consciousness is ego-consciousness. Simply put, if we are not aware of our unbounded status as the witness to creation, we become conscious of our limitations. The QE process leads limited common consciousness to full realization of our inner Self as Eufeeling. When we are aware of Eufeeling and perform action, which we call QE Awareness, that action is the perfect expression of the wholeness we hold in our awareness. In QE Awareness, we don't really feel like we are the performer of the action. Instead, we are more of an observer, watching the actions take place through our body-mind. What is actually happening in QE Awareness is that the role of ego is subdued, while the pure creative forces of life express themselves through us. If you're ready for another corny analogy, it would go something like this. When you experience QE Awareness during your car ride through life, ego is moved to the passenger seat, allowing your Self to take the wheel. There is a kind of schism of awareness. While you identify with ego (that's what ego is: individual identification), you also feel the car is being operated by someone else. In this case, an all-knowing, benevolent driver who knows exactly where he is going and how to get there safely. You can relax and enjoy the ride. As QE Awareness expands and refines over time, you will come to realize that you are both the driver and the passenger, but we'll save that story for another time.

When we lose awareness of Eufeeling, ego moves back into the driver's seat, and all of the concerns of navigating the road of life come rushing back into our consciousness. The joy of the journey is lost in the great effort it takes to stay on the path. Common consciousness has reestablished itself, and ego resumes its frantic search for peace and happiness.

Eufeeling is unbounded, beyond space, time, and death. No thing can destroy Eufeeling, for it is the creator and so is beyond fear. When awareness breaks free of the unbounded anchor of Eufeeling, it becomes localized and individualized. It becomes ego.

Unraveling the Threads of Illusion

Unaware of its unbounded nature, ego feels vulnerable, open to destruction by what it perceives as the foreign forces of cause and effect. Unattached to infinity, ego feels fear for the first time. It is ego against the world, and it must protect itself while at the same time aligning itself with dubious allies in this personal war against death.

Because of its disconnection with pure awareness, ego feels a deep, inner emptiness. It tries to fill this void with the things of its world. It tries to own, and, therefore, control material things like houses, cars, and money. It spends a lot of time trying to control relationships. It falls in love with the power of the mind and manipulates concepts and systems of thought in the hopes of understanding how to fill its inner emptiness. Ego busies itself with frenzied activity, anxiously driving toward more and more. It wants to fill itself to overflowing with anything that will give it comfort. Ego is gluttony at the table of life, whose hunger can never be satiated. Ego feels that if it can collect enough of the stuff of its world, it will eventually feel full and be at peace. This fear-driven decision, based on the perception of insufficiency and inadequacy, is the single cause of human suffering. It is the hub around which every struggling ego revolves on the wheel of karma, the wheel of cause and effect. This primal illusion I call the mistake of the ego.

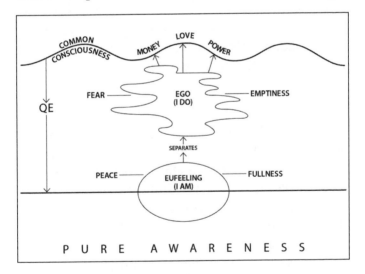

This mistake of the ego drives it ever outward, away from the open arms of pure awareness. Ego feels it must keep swimming, keep its head above the waters of cause and effect. In actuality, it must do the very opposite. To the ego, this is suicide. But once it stops its frantic flailing, ego will sink back into the calm depths of the mind, coming to rest in the fullness of Eufeeling. With awareness of Eufeeling comes the abolition of fear and realization that fullness is its very nature.

Ego is not bad. It is not negative; it is misdirected. Ego is not something we need to eliminate. On the contrary, ego must be expanded until it is infinitely big. Aware of its unbounded status, ego relaxes its tense muscles and slides back over to the passenger's seat. Ready to resume its journey on the road of life, ego serenely settles into its role as ever attentive and grateful witness. Relinquishing control, ego realizes that it was never in control to begin with. And then a profound and beautiful realization dawns. Ego realizes that it never existed beyond the twisted perception of individuality. It gladly accepts that its existence was nothing more than a shadow that dissipated in the loving light of Eufeeling.

If you take pride in your job, that will change. If you fear failure, that will change. If you are happy for any reason, that will change. Every created thing must change. It must be born, traverse its allotted life span, and dissolve back into the fullness from which it came. This is not only the doctrine of the sages but an unalterable law of quantum and classical physics. And in moments of quiet clarity is also our direct observation. Nothing that we know lasts forever. Every *thing* changes; that is, except for change itself.

So, what is the problem of identifying with ego's world of change? If everything is always changing, where do you find stability? How could we ever feel secure when we cannot trust anything to stay the same? Those things that we rely on for security—like other people, employment, money, health, nature, pets—all change. When the thing we rely on for security changes, our security changes. The common conscious mind knows only the ultimate death that change brings. Looking inward, it sees a rushing river of thoughts flowing into a seething sea of emotions. Where is the security in that? Security cannot be built on a constantly shifting and crumbling foundation.

You may have been told that you are responsible for everything that is happening to you. You may believe that your suffering is indeed your fault. But I see this another way. Whether you suffer in this world depends entirely on your perspective. The problem here is that we think we can create a better life for ourselves. This is an illusion. This is the distorted reflection of the mind through ego, not the clear reflection of pure awareness through Eufeeling.

The reason we can't create a better life for ourselves is that it is already perfect. The problem is that we don't recognize that perfection. (This nonrecognition of perfection is actually part of perfection, but that story will take some time to develop and is best saved for a more apropos occasion.) How deeply we believe the illusion is directly related to how strongly we believe we are in control. When we feel that we are in control of things, we are relatively satisfied with ourselves and our position in life. Why try to unravel the mystery of life when you are doing so well, right? The problem is we have to keep close vigil on those forces that would knock us off of our little hill of personal accomplishments and material wealth. The more contentment we feel, the harder we have to work to maintain that illusory sense of inner security. Isn't that true? Mother Nature is ever unraveling the threads of illusion from the fabric of our lives. She is ceaseless in her efforts to awaken us from our slumber, from the dream we call *me*.

When we suffer, we are actually in a better position to see through the illusion of cause and effect. Someone who is suffering knows that what they are doing is not working. They are more likely to give up the idea that they are in control. Unfortunately, in most cases, we turn our attention to how to regain control, plunging us right back into the illusion.

So what is the answer? What are we looking for? If life is not about personal attachments and material wealth, what is it about? Is it a matter of belief and positive thinking? When you see the truth, belief is not necessary, and thinking is in perfect accord with the expression of perception. Life is not about trying to see things in a positive light. Life is the positive light. Ultimately, life is about accepting what is exactly as it is. When that happens, peace descends, and all things are seen in a perfect light. There is no trying needed, only awakening to the reality of what is.

Life Invites Us Along for the Ride

Life follows its own laws and invites us along for the ride. We can appear to be in control and successful for short periods of time, but no one gets what they want all the time. Life will not foster that illusion consistently. It is folly to believe you can. Just look where you are today. Is it anywhere close to where you thought you'd be ten years ago physically, emotionally, economically, spiritually, intellectually, and socially? You may be in the neighborhood of one or two of these areas. You may be better off or worse off than you planned, but one thing is certain: your five-year plan began veering off course the moment you decided you could achieve it. You can row, row, row, your boat gently down the stream, or paddle like a madman against the current, but eventually you will come to realize that you are not in control of the flow, and *life is but a dream.*

If you find yourself resisting this idea, that is ego tugging at your shirtsleeve. This idea may be hard to believe. Stay with me a little longer on this point, and I will offer you an alternative perspective that is not only helpful but a great relief, beyond belief. You don't even have to change your present beliefs. Beliefs don't change our world; Eufeeling does. So, keep your beliefs intact and remain aware of Eufeeling. Awareness of Eufeeling will allow you to keep those beliefs that work and will softly dissolve those that don't ultimately support your best interests. You will soon come to realize that belief is a relative player in the game of life. The knowledge I am offering you can be experienced to its fullest whether you believe in it or not.

You have to ask yourself why people who are totally unprepared can succeed while others fail despite impeccable preparation and potential. We invent rationalizations like luck and karma to explain our inability to control success and failure. These belief systems help us to explain away our constant and daily observation that we are not in control of our lives. We might say someone is lucky or that they have good karma, but the fact remains that consistent success is beyond the control of even those of us who are most prepared. In actuality, life, the forces that germinate and guide our world from the lowly amoeba to the majestic motion of the galaxies, is in control. When we harmonize with those forces, life becomes an effortless flow. When we fight them, living becomes a struggle. If we don't learn that single lesson and continue to paddle against the flow of life, struggle turns into just one more of the infinite varieties of suffering. What life has in store for us is never what we think. Our thinking is rarely grand enough. Life has more to offer us than we can imagine. So, the best idea is to stop struggling with the idea that you know what is best for you and the rest of the world, and let life take the wheel. A little later, you will learn how to do just that. You will be amazed.

What We Perceive We Believe

Many say that we can change our lives if we believe we can. As I mentioned before, belief has nothing to do with it. It is a matter of perception, nothing more. What we perceive we believe. "Well, Frank," you say, "I know that if I strongly believe something, in time, I will begin to perceive that as true." Yes, this is true, but only partly so. It appears we have a chicken and egg conundrum here. There is the old dictum "seeing is believing." You could just as easily say, "Believing is seeing." Any expression of prejudice is a perfect illustration of seeing what you believe. The example that most readily springs to mind is racial prejudice, and we have more than enough examples of that both past and present. If you believe an individual from a particular race or socioeconomic group or gender less capable, intelligent, motivated, or friendly, you will most assuredly look for and find behavior to support your beliefs. So, how do we untangle this belief-perception predicament? The answer is quite simple.

We can think of it in terms of cause and effect. If a strong wind blows over a tree, we can say that the wind was the cause and the falling tree was the effect. If we then ask what caused the strong wind, we could say heat rising from the ocean mixing with cold air from above. If we follow this reasoning and ask what caused the ocean to heat up, we could say the sun. What caused the sun? Hydrogen fusion. What causes the hydrogen? Atoms. What causes atoms? Subatomic particles. What causes subatomic particles? Wave energy. What causes wave energy? Zero point (physics term for Eufeeling). What causes zero point? Implicate order (physics term for pure awareness). What causes implicate order or pure awareness? Nothing causes pure awareness. It has no form and is, therefore, uncreated and without cause.

If you were to pick any occurrence in the middle of this chain of events, would you be choosing a cause or effect? The answer is, whichever you want it to be. For instance, hydrogen fusion is both a cause and an effect. It is the cause of the sun's radiation that heated the ocean. But hydrogen fusion is also an effect of the protons and electrons that form hydrogen atoms. If you were looking for hydrogen fusion to be a cause, you would be right. You would also be right if you wanted to find it to be an effect. Cause and effect are a matter of relative perception.

We can apply the same logic to belief and perception. You can pick any single event throughout the never-ending chain of perception influencing belief, influencing perception, influencing belief ad infinitum.

The event will be seen as caused by perception or belief depending on the position you want to support.

If you need money to pay the rent, you perceive the need for money and, depending on your options, would believe or doubt that you will get the rent money. Your belief in success or failure depends on your perception of the options presented to you. You could work more hours, borrow the money, steal the money, or bend the forces of nature to your will by doing subtle energy work or affirmations. Based on your perception, you will choose the option that you believe will most effectively provide you with the rent money. Once you secure the money for your rent, you will perceive that the process was successful and believe that it will work the same way for you in the future. Do you see how belief and perception are intimately related? They inspire each other. They work together. But just like hydrogen fusion was in the middle of the chain of causes and effects that knocked down your tree, belief and perception are two sides of the same coin.

We appear to be caught in a relative roundabout from which there is no exit. But we don't see it as circular. We think that cause and effect, belief and perception events are linear. That is only because we are too close to the problem. Here's what I mean.

If we take a long walk along a flat surface, it looks like we are walking in a straight line. In actuality, we are not walking in a straight line, but, instead, we are walking along the curve of the earth. Because the earth is so huge and our senses do not perceive the curvature of the earth while we are walking on it, we think we are walking on a flat surface in a straight line. From the perspective of outer space, we step back from our limited, linear perception on earth and can easily see that the earth's surface is curved. It is this ultimate perception outside the limited framework of our linear-locked mind that frees us from misconceptions, confusion, and suffering.

You might well say, "If I believe the earth is curved, I will act accordingly and so do not actually have to perceive the curvature of the earth." This is a very good observation. And it works very well until your walk on a flat surface changes. Remember your mind, the belief-perception playground, perceives only change. There are no straight lines in nature. Your mind cannot pursue the illusion of a straight line indefinitely. That is against its very nature. Your mind must focus on what is changing. In our straight-line analogy, your mind would take up mountain climbing. It will relish in the exploration of peaks and valleys and caves. To your mind, it is pretty hard to maintain a belief in a gently curving world when you are climbing straight up the face of a mountain.

You see, if life went in a straight line, we would all have all the answers. Our problems are the mountains and valleys of our lives. Because we are so close to our problems, be they financial, spiritual, or otherwise, we do not get beyond the cause and effect, belief-perceptual overview. We plan our life in a straight line and think that we can control the cause and effect that has been unfolding since time began. We think we can do it by changing our belief or perception. It just doesn't work that way, and it takes a lot of effort and belief to convince ourselves that it does. It takes a huge amount of energy to believe what is not true.

But there is a way free of this apparent deterministic prison of cause and effect. Like the ability to float free comes effortlessly when we travel beyond the earth's gravity, all the inherent contradictions of life resolve themselves when we are able to travel beyond the linear, cause and effect perceptions imposed on us by day-to-day living. How is this accomplished? I'm so glad you asked.

As far as our analogy goes, you already know how to float beyond the confines of Earth's gravity, gaining you an outer-worldview, an unbounded perspective of the whole. If the earth were your mind, pure awareness would be the nothingness of outer space. Eufeeling would be you orbiting in unbounded space while observing that beautiful blue sphere we call home. The QE process is the spaceship that bore you beyond the binding effect of gravity. Floating unfettered from Earth's gravity, beyond the influence of the cause and effect world below, you would be free to marvel at the earth's diversity and beauty untouched by her violence.

A Fly in the Cosmic Web of Creation

When you do QE and become aware of Eufeeling, you become aware of your Self at the seat of creation. From this exalted place, you do not create but are the ultimate observer, surveying all of creation as it unfolds from you. The Vedas, ancient Indian scriptures, liken this to a cosmic spider, drawing thread from inside itself to weave the web of life. The fly that is snared in this phenomenal web of cause and effect is ego, the limited perception of me with all its ideas, hopes, fears, and beliefs. The more it struggles to free itself, the more entangled in the web of life it becomes. As ego intensifies its efforts to be free, its struggling draws the attention of spider Eufeeling. Finally, and with infinite compassion,

Eufeeling!

Eufeeling consumes ego, assimilating its consciousness into its own body. Expanded beyond the bounds of its limited vision, ego dissolves into the oneness of the Spinner and observes as She moves on to the next fly.

The ultimate realization is that life is perfect exactly as it is. There is an underlying and ultimate harmony that permeates all creation. Of this, there is no doubt. Everything is just as it is. Of this, there is no doubt. Disharmony is the result of seeing the parts without the perception of the whole. You could say that disharmony is the result of tunnel vision.

Let's see what would happen if you were to take an empty paper towel roll and hold it up to your eye and then were to place the other end of the tube a few inches away from a painting hanging in a museum. Next, listen to someone who is standing several feet from the painting with both eyes open describe what they see. Compare what they see to what you see. With a tremor in their voice, they describe majestic blue mountains, cool green forests, and the golden meadow stippled with splashes of sunlight slashing through low-hanging rain clouds. They say the painting fills them with awe. When asked to describe what you see and feel, you respond, "I see a blob of brown with a gray smudge running through it. I feel I am missing something." No matter how hard you try, you will not be able to see the beauty or feel the joy that they described. Your perspective is limited. Now you can say, "I don't like brown with gray smudges. I'm going to change my perspective." So, you move the tube to another point on the painting. Here you see gold and blue, and these colors are more enjoyable for you. You say, "Yes, I now know the joy that you have described. Blue and gold are much better than brown and gray." But your belief is based on a limited perspective. Blue and gold soon lose their charm, and you move the empty tube to another and yet another point on the painting. Your belief is that if you work your way around to enough points on the painting, you can eventually put them all together and will finally be able to perceive the whole picture. Of course, the pieces can never add up to the synergy of the whole. Following your belief, you will continue to collect the pieces of the painting until the museum lights go out.

What do you have to do to see the complete painting? I'll tell you: *nothing!* That's right, absolutely nothing. If you are complete in your non-doing, you will stop thinking about what you must do next, your body will become completely relaxed, and the empty tube will merely fall from your hand. Spontaneously and without effort, you will behold the painting in its entirety. From this simple act of letting go, you will experience for yourself the awe and beauty once described to you by others with expanded vision.

Appreciating wholeness is the perception of perfection. No amount of belief or limited perception can make this happen. It is only by letting go and appreciating what appears before you, as it is, that the astounding simplicity of perfection will dawn in your awareness. Your apparent control over the pieces of your life, like moving the tube from one point on the painting to another, is an illusion. It is the dissatisfaction of where you are that spurs you to move to the next point. No point or collection of points in your life can ever add up to the appreciation, wonder, and admiration of a single glimpse of the perfection inherent in your world. Just as the perfection of the painting was always present, so the perfection of this life is always present. There is nothing you need to do other than open your eyes to the beauty of your Self, and that is as easy as letting an empty tube fall from your hand. Soon, you will learn QE Intention founded on this single point: the less you do the more perfection will be reflected in your life. Do nothing, and the perception of perfection will dawn beyond belief.

Main Points for Chapter 9

- When individual awareness expands to universal awareness, individual action is guided by universal wisdom.

- The mistake of the ego: Because of its disconnection with pure awareness, ego feels a deep inner emptiness. It turns away from Eufeeling and tries to fill this void with the things of its world.

- Whether you suffer in this world depends entirely on your perspective.

- The reason we can't create a better life for ourselves is that it is already perfect. The problem is that we don't recognize that perfection.

- Our belief systems help us to explain away our constant and daily observation that we are not in control of our lives.

- When you do QE and become aware of Eufeeling, you become aware of your Self at the seat of creation.

- The ultimate realization is that life is perfect exactly as it is.

- Appreciating wholeness is the perception of perfection.

- The less you do, the more perfection will be reflected in your life. Do nothing, and the perception of perfection will dawn beyond belief.

CHAPTER 10

Perfect Perception

"If the doors of perception were cleansed everything would appear to man as it is, infinite."

— WILLIAM BLAKE

A Matter of Perspective

We humans evolved under very specific conditions under very narrow circumstances. Think about it: we inhabit an incredibly narrow slice of this universe. In terms of our physical presence, we exist about midway between the atom and the galaxy. Our minds can comprehend neither the vastness of a galaxy nor the micro-minute distance between atoms. The conditions on our home world are also somewhat middling. For instance, we exist in an extremely narrow temperature range. Just beyond our front door, in outer space, temperatures approach absolute zero. How cold is that? Absolute zero is -459.67°F (-273.15°C). As I remember it, that's almost as cold as the Januaries I spent in Michigan. Contrast the temperature of outer space to that of the center of the sun at 27 million °F (50 million °C), which approaches our summers here in South Florida. Of course, I'm kidding. The extremes right here on the surface of the earth are in the neighborhood of 136°F (57.8°C) down to a -129°F (-89°C), with the average temperature of the earth being around 60°F (15°C). When you compare the celestial extremes to the ones here on Earth, you can appreciate how precarious is our position. A minor shift in either direction, and all the stories of all the humans that live, or have ever lived, dissolve back into the atoms from which they spring.

Our ability to perceive our environment is likewise limited to an extremely narrow range of sensory input. Our senses pick up only the grossest manifestations of creation. If you wrap your knuckles on a table, the table looks and feels solid. But physics knows that table is almost entirely without substance. Vibrating waves, subatomic particles, molecules, and so on give the appearance of solidity, just as the blades of a rapidly spinning fan look solid. We interact with our world based on how we perceive it.

Following is an analogy of gravity. It demonstrates the difference in perspective between Newtonian physics and Einstein's general relativity. But more than that, it reveals how perception influences our thinking. We can draw a parallel between Newtonian physics and normal sensory perception. Generally speaking, Newton's laws reflect life on the normal sensory level of touch, sight, hearing, and so on. Relativity and quantum mechanics, on the other hand, describe forces that govern the very large and the very small, beyond the reach of normal human sensory perception.

We all know that gravity is a force that attracts. A bigger body, like the sun, will attract to it a smaller body, like the earth. The larger Earth will attract smaller things to it, like water and rocks and people. Throw a rock in the air and then run for cover, because you know that the earth's gravity will pull it back to the earth. In actuality, gravity is not an attractive force like magnetism. Smaller objects are actually pushed toward larger objects by space-time. It sounds confusing, I know, but that is only because we are used to thinking of gravity as an attractive force. We can see things being *drawn* to the earth, and we can feel gravity in our own bodies. The push of space and time is far more abstract. But this simple illustration will shift your perception 180° and free you from the misconception that gravity attracts.

Let's say you were looking down from a ten-story window. Directly below you is a large round object, sitting in the middle of a rectangle. Next, you see a man approach the outer edge of the rectangle. He places a small object on the inside edge of the rectangle. When he lets go, the small object is immediately attracted to the large object in the middle of the rectangle. Your first thought is that the large round object is a magnet, and the small object must be made of iron.

When you take the elevator to the ground floor and step outside, you see that the rectangular object is actually a trampoline. Sitting in the middle of the trampoline is not a magnet but a common, everyday Lucite bowling ball. The small object turns out to be a glass marble. Your first thought is, *How can Lucite attract glass?* Then you notice that the weight of the bowling ball has created a deep depression in the trampoline. You then pick up the marble and place it at the edge of the trampoline. When you let go of the marble, it performs exactly as you observed when looking down from ten stories above. The marble rolls directly toward the bowling ball until it hits it. You now know that the marble was not attracted to the bowling ball but was pushed toward the bowling ball because the outside of the trampoline was higher than the depression in the middle. If the trampoline were level, the marble would not move toward the bowling ball at all.

Larger objects, like planets, push down or distort what is referred to as the *fabric* of space-time, just like the bowling ball caused a depression in the fabric of the trampoline. It was Einstein who discovered that gravity is actually a pushing force, and this single cognition, along with the advent of quantum mechanics, revolutionized the field of physics. As a result of this shift in perspective, we have experienced a technological insurrection that has touched literally every life on this planet.

Not all humans are bound strictly to their senses. There are those special individuals whose senses are able to perceive beyond the solidity of everyday objects. All humans are equipped to perceive beyond the gross sensory level. In some, extrasensory perception needs to be developed, while others come by it naturally. They are able to see, hear, and feel subtler energies than usual. Among these people with refined sensual acuity, you will find energy healers and medical intuitives, those who communicate with disincarnate masters, angels, and other subtle entities, shamans, yogis, and many others who are esoterically talented. These sensitive people can appear to perform miracles when seen by those whose senses dwell only on the obvious. To the mind that perceives through the everyday, ordinary senses, these people seem strangely out of place, yet their value cannot be denied.

Knowledge Is Ignorance

No matter what you perceive, whether it is in your environment or in your mind, your perception is flawed. Perception can never be 100 percent accurate. No two people see the world in exactly the same way. This was also a revelation of Einstein's. People are separated by time and space, which makes every individual perspective different from every other. Likewise, no two people can have the same knowledge and, therefore, the same comprehension. Complete agreement with another is delusion. You may believe that you are in perfect agreement with another person, but you only have to delve more deeply into your beliefs and perceptions. and you will quickly find a point at which your thinking diverges from theirs. Have you ever thought you and a friend were in perfect agreement on an issue only to find you completely misunderstood each other? When it comes right down to it, each of us lives within a cocoon spun from the threads of our own individual perceptions and beliefs. Now, I know this all sounds pretty dreary, but that is an illusion as well. Above the clouds, the sun is ever shining.

Except for a few rare individuals in every generation, suffering has dogged the heels of the human race from the beginning of our recorded history. In fact, a closer look at our progress through the ages can be a pretty accurate analogy for individual progress through life. Every age of human development looks on the one before it as being less developed. For the most part, they have felt that they were living truths that previous generations had failed to realize. For instance, a primitive witch doctor may have treated the common viral cold as an infestation of an evil spirit and used herbs and incantations to drive out the unwanted entity. The patient would be free of the symptoms of the invading guest in about ten days. As medical treatment evolved, the physician may have introduced the latest technology of bloodletting. If the patient didn't lose too much blood, he recovered from the cold in ten days and several weeks later, felt rejuvenated by the newly generated blood cells promulgating through his veins. Today's common cold victim is treated with the latest antibiotics, antihistamines, and nighttime sleep concoctions. Recovery time . . . ten days. Recovery from the decimated gastrointestinal flora brought on by the antibacterial therapy will take weeks to months, opening the patient to a plethora of secondary diseases and conditions, along with a heightened immunity to antibiotics, further opening the door to the proliferation of superbugs and an inevitable worldwide epidemic. Right now, herbs and incantations are looking pretty darn good.

On average, it took the ancient hunter gatherer about three and a half days a week of hunting and gathering to survive. That's a 28-hour workweek. Compare that to the 50-, 60-, and 70-hour workweeks of modern man, with all his labor-saving devices and advanced communication and related technology. Now, help me understand how that qualifies as the *progress* we keep bragging about. Despite our fantastic advances in communication, we have become increasingly more isolated as individuals.

I make these points for this reason: Our perception of progress has created a belief that we are better off than our ancient and even more recent forefathers. It encourages us to continue in the same direction that we have been going, even though our lives are becoming more hectic, chaotic, and isolated. Deep within each of us is an emerging sense of urgency. Most of us turn away from this inner urging, and when it persists, we bludgeon it senseless with drugs and alcohol, hours of television, overwork, sexual promiscuity and deviancy, and all the other aberrancies we have come to accept as normal. Ideals like fair play, charity, compassion, and community pride are looked on as weakness in this exceptionally competitive world. Our belief that we are progressing overrules even our common sense. What sane society could take an objective look at what we are doing to ourselves and our environment and call it progress?

As goes the parts so goes the whole. The society is a reflection of the individuals who make it up. That means each of us is adding to the problem. We have missed the point. It is not a matter of belief versus perception. The root of the problem is that we believe our perceptions as accurate and true representations of the world in which we live. This simply is not the case. It's easy for us to look at our governments, communities, or even our families and point out the obvious insanity by which they function. It's much harder to see that same lunacy manifesting in our own lives. With very rare exception, self-destructive behavior is alive and thriving in each of us. But don't throw in the towel just yet. I wouldn't accentuate the negative if I didn't have a working plan to enhance the positive. Or more accurately, like the veritable white lotus rising out of the fetid slime, show you how to be free of both negativity and positivity.

Earlier, we introduced the idea that belief and perception are two sides of the same coin. Whichever one we choose to champion depends on how we interpret our little corner of the cause and effect universe. Some believe that belief is king, and others perceive perception to be the answer. In the end, it really doesn't matter, for we have the know-how to move beyond these mental fisticuffs.

In the belief versus perception debate, it is perception that wins. But before you perception people break out the noisemakers and champagne, let me qualify. There is another kind of perception not tied to the field of change, the field of death. It is the one that will usher joy, love, and compassion into our lives. The perception that frees us from the field of death is the perception of the essence of life, that ultimate perception of Eufeeling.

If you have been doing the exercises I suggested and have been enjoying QE Awareness over the last few days, you will have begun to see subtle changes taking place in your life. Let's take a few minutes to discover how that is happening.

First, during the time that you are sitting with Eufeeling, do you notice an easy relaxation in your body and a clear stillness in your mind? At times, while sitting quietly, you may feel peace or bliss or lightheartedness. How about light and lazy thoughts that seem to almost whisper so as not to disturb your inner peace? Are they accompanied with a sense that everything is all right just as it is?

During your daily activity, what do you notice that is different? Are you less excitable, less irritable, or less angry? Do other drivers bother you less? Do you feel more rested and clear? Have you noticed that nature is more alive and bad weather more tolerable? Sleeping better, food tastes better, less tired at the end of the day? What else have you noticed?

During conversations with others, are you less distracted and listening with real interest? Are you less impatient to say what you want to say, more comfortable to just be who you are? Have you had more positive feelings, like compassion or understanding for others' predicaments? These and others are the symptoms of stepping outside your cause and effect world and becoming aware of Eufeeling. You didn't need to do anything for these changes to take place. They happened without effort simply because you are aware of Eufeeling. Absolutely nothing more is needed.

As you continue this simple practice along with the QE Intention, which you will soon learn, subtle yet powerful changes will take place in your life. Just as the changes you have enjoyed so far have come innocently and without effort, so will the major remodeling of your life unfold. Eufeeling will satisfy your desires even before they become conscious. The result will be an inner confidence and grace emanating from a knowing that everything is perfect just as it is. From this foundation of fullness, and in response to QE Intention, you will begin to receive material gifts to garnish your material yearnings. Like first drawing an arrow fully in the opposite direction from the target, it is the withdrawing from life that prepares us for our most dynamic interaction with it. If we are to fulfill our desires, we start by drawing common consciousness fully to the silent depths of the mind where Eufeeling awaits. How is that done? I'll save that for the next chapter.

Main Points for Chapter 10

- Our ability to perceive our environment is limited to an extremely narrow range of sensory input.

- There are those special individuals whose senses are able to perceive beyond the solidity of everyday objects.

- No two people see the world in exactly the same way. They cannot have the same perception, and they cannot share the same knowledge.

- Suffering has dogged the heels of the human race from the beginning of our recorded history.

- Our perception of progress has created a belief that we are better off than our ancient and even more recent forefathers. This is an illusion.

- The perception that frees us from the field of death is the perception of the essence of life, that ultimate perception of Eufeeling.

CHAPTER 11

Desire

*"Desire without knowledge is not good, and one who
moves too hurriedly misses the way."*

— PROVERBS 19:2

Desire: A Boon and a Bane

Ah desire! How the mind lights up when it hears
that word. Desire excites the imagination and prepares
the body for pleasure. Desire creates a spur to action. It is
the quest to fulfill desire that drives humankind to delve
the deepest waters, ascend the highest peaks, and dream
beyond the stars. Desire is the great motivator and the
cause of many sleepless nights. Driven by desire, we
launch wars, cure disease, build societies, and explore
the depths of the human soul.

Desire is both a boon and a bane: a boon when it is
satisfied and a bane when it isn't. All life moves away
from pain and toward pleasure. It is desire that provides

both the inspiration and motivation to move beyond our limitations and fill our greatest potential.

The word *desire* elicits many degrees of intensity. It is most commonly thought of as a strong wish. *The American Heritage Dictionary of the English Language, 4th edition,* informs us that desire is to wish or long for something. Synonyms include covet, crave, or want. A very strong expression of desire would be lust. Lust is desire gone awry and could be considered unhealthy. The spectrum of desire can range from a light tickle in the back of our minds to an overwhelming obsession that drives us to destruction.

Let's say that you feel thirst. Your initial impulse is to drink water. There is no particular emotion attached to that impulse. If you are denied water for a few minutes, you may find you mind moving on to other things, confident your thirst will be quenched in due time. Still no noticeable emotion attached to the impulse to quench your thirst. But if you are denied water for a couple of days, you will come to crave water to stave off death from dehydration. Now you will experience a very strong desire. That means the original impulse to find water changes, and so do the emotions. The impulse becomes more dominant and direct and the emotions stronger. Instead of a leisurely stroll through the park, your thirst drives you headlong into the lake to quench your thirst. Result: Impulse ends, desire satisfied, deep emotional release.

The Desire Complex

When we have a desire, it is always part of what I call the desire complex. The desire complex has three parts to it: the desire, the object of desire, and the condition. The object is not limited to a person, place, or thing. It can just as easily be a mental form like an idea, dream, philosophy, another desire, or even the desire to be free of desire. That one is usually a strong one with many tendrils to bind its owner to the ever-turning wheel of the desire complex.

The condition includes the situation or the circumstances that we need to overcome in order to obtain the object. For instance, if you want to own (desire) a shiny red sports car (the object), you must overcome the obstacles or circumstances (the condition) that stand between you and owning the sports car. In this case, in order to satisfy the condition you might need to find a reputable dealer, test drive several models to see which will best suit your needs, earn the money or apply for financing, and since your shiny red sports car only has two seats, convince your wife that your three children, two dogs, and parakeet will fit quite comfortably somewhere in the trunk.

The condition will be met when you satisfy all the necessary elements involved. In the case of owning the shiny red sports car, it would be finding the right car, financing, and schmoozing your wife. Once the condition is satisfied and you have obtained the object, your desire will be extinguished and you will be at peace—at least until the next desire pops into your mind, and you decide to trade in your shiny red sports car for a glass-bottom fishing boat.

Before we go a step further, let's do a little experiment to help us better understand how desire, the emotions attached to an impulse, affects us emotionally.

Exercise: Getting and Losing

After reading this exercise, lay down your book, close your eyes, and follow the instructions.

With eyes closed, think about something that you really, really want. Think of something that you desire with all your heart. Note how you feel when you think about the possibility of getting this object of desire. You might feel excitement or hope or even nervousness about getting it. Take a moment to register your feelings.

Now imagine that you actually have gotten what you desire and note how your feelings change. Your anticipation and hopefulness may be replaced with the joy of achievement or contentment or even pride. You see a shift in the kind and quality of your emotions.

Now imagine that what you have is abruptly taken away from you. Note how you feel when you lose what you had. Your emotions most probably take a turn toward the negative. You may feel a sense of loss or sorrow or perhaps frustration and even anger.

The Secret of Suffering

What does this simple exercise teach us? Something that when observed on the surface seems obvious and even innocent, but once we take a more discerning look can be quite alarming. On the surface, we recognize that emotions accompany desire and that our emotions change with the circumstances. They are different when we want something, different still when we get something, and change again when we lose something. But hidden beneath the obvious is something much more sinister, which we will find out is the cause of underlying restlessness, worry, and chronic dissatisfaction. We are about to discover the secret of suffering: the seed of disharmony and discontent.

We have traditionally taken this approach. That is, we feel the need to reach out and pluck the object of our desire for our very own. We overcome the various elements standing in our way and then feel the exuberant joy of finally reaching the goal or owning the object. That seems logical. Just get what you want and eliminate the pricking of that uncomfortable thorn we call desire. Unfortunately, securing the object is only a temporary fix. As soon as one desire is quelled, another rises to take its place. Isn't that true? After a brief interlude where we feel a kind of relative quiet, a mellow satisfaction in our minds, we again become restless and are soon off on another quest to quell desire.

In affluent countries, many if not most of our desires are for things we want but do not absolutely need. Think about it. Do we really need a cappuccino machine; a quadruple-bladed razor; a 52-inch TV; designer jeans; 12 pairs of shoes (I'm being very conservative here—some individuals amass scores of pairs of shoes . . . you know who you are); a shiny red sports car; or a double mocha latte with an extra shot of decaf espresso, whipped cream, and chocolate sprinkles? If you doubt me, take a quick look in your closet, kitchen, or garage, and note all the items lying about that you desired, obtained, and are now not using. Some may still have the price tag on them. Our common experience is that shortly after we satisfy our craving for an object, it loses its appeal. We can desire things that we need and things that we don't need. That's obvious. The fruits of life are meant to be eaten. Who doesn't feel better watching a little TV, wearing new clothes, or going out to dinner with friends? It is not the usefulness of a desire that we are concerned with here. What is more important is why a desire forms and if it can be satisfied in a more practical, even more prevailing way.

It appears that the object has the power to remove desire, but upon closer inspection, we find this simply is not true. Well, forgive me. It is true in a superficial sense. But there seems to be a deeper underlying desire from which we are never completely liberated. That desire is the source, the progenitor, of all other desires. That basic desire is the head of Medusa, that mythological monster with snakes for hair, who turns you to stone by only looking in your eyes. The lesser desires are the snakes, wriggling and writhing, hard to grab, and harder to hold. Cut off the head of one snake, as the fable goes, and two more take its place. You have probably noticed in your own life that if you satisfy one desire, two more take its place. The only way to completely rid yourself of all those pesky varmints is to cut off the head of Medusa. Following through with our analogy, that would mean finding and fulfilling that deepest, most basic desire.

When we acquire the object of desire, we extinguish the fire of desire. (Hey! I made it rhyme! I just love poetry, don't you?) We look at the object as if it has the power to put out that fire. The object becomes the focus of our efforts and if not consciously, certainly subconsciously, it is elevated to the exalted position of desire slayer. But that is all illusion.

Have you ever noticed that as soon as you reach a goal—get a raise, buy a house, win an award, or fall in romantic love—the good feeling just doesn't last? Why is that? Why can't we stay satisfied for long? Objects, people, organizations, philosophies, and dreams are a relative fascination. They are Medusa's mesmerizing snakes, distracting your mind from the reality of life. Most people go from one thing to another all their lives, searching for that ultimate happiness. When we are driven by desire, we can never rest; that is, until we die. Outward goals lead away from inner peace. That is why we fail to find lasting satisfaction in relative matters. We are meant to realize the ultimate matter, as it were, Eufeeling. Eufeeling is the ultimate goal. It brings with it the dissolution of desire as a motivating entity. Eufeeling is the death of desire.

Okay, I can't help myself. I have to take the Medusa analogy a little further. As the story goes, Perseus beheaded Medusa. He grabbed her head by the snake-hair and held it up. Oddly enough, the snakes don't die, but they are unable to harm. When we are aware of Eufeeling, we still have desires, but they cannot grab hold of us; they cannot constrict our minds with harmful emotions. What we want ultimately is to be at peace, free to sail the ocean of universal love without being buffeted by constant waves of desires. We want to be free of the desire for love. We want to love just for the sake of love. We want to be free of reason or circumstance or need. Living in QE Awareness desires are no more than delightful dalliances, gentle ripples on the vast ocean of bliss we call Eufeeling. There, one can love a leaf and a rock and a person with the same intensity. In QE Awareness, we look Medusa squarely in the eyes and know that universal love abides where fear once lived.

The Solution to Suffering

When we are aware of Eufeeling, the fulfillment of one desire doesn't create a desire for more. You already have more than most when you are aware of Eufeeling. QE Awareness breaks the desire-action-desire cycle, because it satisfies the primal desire to feel whole and beyond harm. Now the desire for a red sports car is just a blip on your emotional radar screen, a ripple on the ocean of wholeness. If you own unbounded wholeness, owning a sports car is really a minor matter. After the initial desire-ripple passes, the ocean of wholeness remains still.

Let's now create a simple experience to emphasize this point.

Experience: Give It All Away

Imagine that your imagination can create anything you want, anytime, in unlimited quantities. Imagine getting all the things you have ever desired: food, money, friends, possessions, respect. Take time to develop a strong image, feeling emotions and using sight, smell, touch, hearing, and taste around the things that you create. Now that you can have anything you want, give it all away. Give it to poor people, friends, rich people, your teacher, mother, child. Giving away what you have is easy, because you know you can imagine more. It is not only easy to give when you have an unlimited supply it's also fun. It feels good. Giving from infinite resources frees you from the need to hold on. It frees you from the feeling of deficiency and needs and the desires they draw to them.

Every created thing enters this world through Eufeeling. If there were ever a field of infinite resources, Eufeeling is it. Become aware of Eufeeling in just the right way, and all the forces of creation will mobilize on your behalf. This is what I call QE Intention. When you have a QE Intention, you become aware of the unbounded fullness that you are. Your desires are tenderly hushed, like crying babes in the arms of mother Eufeeling. Then the unbounded organizing influence of Eufeeling begins to bring order to your life. In complete harmony and free from the chaos of so many distracting desires, you will come to realize great satisfaction on the material plane as well.

QE Intention is natural. It is the way we were meant to be: free to enjoy the fullness of our bountiful world. Before we learn how to have a QE Intention, it will be good to get a bit of a deeper understanding of how QE Intention works. In the next chapter, you will be introduced to the forces that come into play to support your wishes and fulfill your deepest desires. In the meantime, continue to do QE on a regular basis, and slip into QE Awareness as often as feels comfortable throughout the day. As you bring together your experience and your understanding of Eufeeling, you are preparing your mind to revel in the delicate, delicious joys of the QE Intention.

Eufeeling!

Main Points for Chapter 11

- It is desire that provides both the inspiration and motivation to move beyond our limitations and fulfill our greatest potential.

- As soon as one desire is quelled, another rises to take its place.

- Most people go from one thing to another all their lives, searching for that ultimate happiness.

- Outward goals lead away from inner peace.

- Eufeeling is the death of desire.

- When we are aware of Eufeeling, the fulfillment of one desire doesn't create a desire for more. Eufeeling is the primal goal for every desire.

- Become aware of Eufeeling in just the right way, and all the forces of creation will mobilize on your behalf.

The Art of QE Intention

"God is not attained by a process of addition to anything in the soul, but by a process of subtraction."

— MEISTER ECKEHART

Pure Eufeeling

If you have followed through with my suggestions, you will have been spending a good deal of time enfolded in the tender arms of Eufeeling. You will have, at times, felt a very still, deep, calm within both your mind and your body. At times, you may have felt like you were deep asleep except that your mind was wide awake. Longer periods of sitting with Eufeeling encourage this kind of profound inner wakefulness. It comes quickly and naturally just by doing QE with eyes closed.

This state of inner wakefulness, of absolute stillness in your mind, cannot be forced. Just as a reminder, you cannot try in any way to *create* this innocent condition of ultimate rest. So, when you do QE sitting quietly with your eyes closed, make sure you are not trying, or even anticipating, what will come next. This is important, so be sure you make a mental note of it: Your only focus is to be aware of Eufeeling. Let me repeat that: Your only focus is to be aware of Eufeeling. Actually, "focus" is too strong a word here. Shifting from thoughts to Eufeeling is more of an intent or impulse than a focusing. When you are not aware of Eufeeling, just the *impulse* to have it will bring Eufeeling effortlessly back into your awareness.

If Eufeeling is not there, you will either have thoughts or no thoughts. If you have thoughts, they will most likely be very quiet, indistinct thoughts that lazily come and go. When you notice that you are having thoughts, you will also notice you are having a good feeling at the same time. At that point, you very softly pay intention to that good feeling. You see, you just effortlessly switch your awareness from thoughts to Eufeeling. With just the slightest impulse, you become aware of Eufeeling. Let's do this: Think of a car (I'll wait) . . . now think of a house . . . and now think of a flower. Note how naturally and easily your mind moves from one thought to another. That is just how easily you become aware of Eufeeling. That is all there is to it. It is just allowing the thought to be aware of Eufeeling to take place. If you are having no thoughts, which is the non-experience of pure awareness, you won't know it until you start thinking again or are aware of Eufeeling. In either case, you already know what to do then: easily become aware of Eufeeling.

There is a variation of being aware of Eufeeling. It is a very subtle perception of Eufeeling called *Pure Eufeeling.*

This state is characterized by awareness of no thoughts but shouldn't be confused with pure awareness. When you are experiencing pure awareness, you are not aware of it *at the time.* It is a non-experience or lack of experience. You only know you were in pure awareness after you are out of it and your mind starts thinking again. You recognize it as a gap in your thinking, a period of non-experience.

Pure Eufeeling is the most refined awareness you can have. It is a perception of pure awareness and Eufeeling simultaneously. Pure Eufeeling means that you perceive Eufeeling before it reflects any form or feelings, like joy or peace or bliss, in your mind. I only mention it here, because you might confuse it with the nonthinking, pure awareness state. You can tell Pure Eufeeling from pure awareness because you are aware of it at the time you experience it. You know you are aware, but what you are aware of is nothing.

- *Pure Eufeeling:* Aware that you are aware of nothing while you are having it

- *Pure Awareness:* Not aware until you start thinking again, and you realize that there was a "gap" in your thinking

Either experience is not a goal. When you have Pure Eufeeling, you have no goals, only observation of what is reflecting in your mind. For what we are doing now, it doesn't matter whether you are aware of thoughts, Eufeeling, or pure awareness. Your interaction is still the same, innocent observation of the remarkable machinery of creation as it unfolds on the screen of Pure Eufeeling.

People who can create miracles and materialize things out of thin air do so from the level of Pure Eufeeling. Christ created from this level when he performed his miracles. When he turned water to wine and materialized the fishes and loaves, his intentions sprang directly from a firmly founded awareness of the basic creative force of nature. Having an intention from Pure Eufeeling is like bringing a magnet in close proximity to iron filings sprinkled randomly on a piece of paper. As the magnet is moved closer to the scattered filings, they begin to move in what appears to be chaotic fashion. But once the magnet touches the bottom of the paper, the filings are lined up in perfect order. The closer the magnet gets to the filings, the more order they exhibit. The more established one's awareness is in Pure Eufeeling, the more order is reflected in their lives. Even if chaos appears to dominate, it is only the dance of the iron filings before the magnet. In Pure Eufeeling, the perception of perfection dawns quickly, making sense of an otherwise chaotic world.

Pure Eufeeling is the most pure perception. There is no distortion, no ego to disrupt the clean expression of this impulse of purity. In common consciousness, our thoughts are like waves dashed on the rocky shores of reality, exploding in a spray of chaos and criticism driven before the prevailing winds of cause and effect. In the deepest level of your mind, no such conflict can exist. So, when you have a thought or desire, it is immediately fulfilled. This is most amazing! You can have anything you want while you are experiencing Pure Eufeeling.

For instance, if you have the impulse to taste an apple while aware of Pure Eufeeling, immediately the apple takes form in your mind, and your emotions and senses vividly respond. On this level, you can appreciate the apple fully, even more fully than the actual eating of an apple in common consciousness. If you eat an apple in common consciousness, your mind is elsewhere, and you miss the sound of breaking the apple skin with your teeth, the spray of juice against your lips, and the flood of succulent sour-sweet meat arousing in you one of the greatest pleasures on Earth. Instead, you chomp and talk and swallow, almost without remembering that you ate an apple at all.

Do you remember the movie projector analogy used earlier? We said that Eufeeling was the lens and the film in the movie projector. The pure light (pure awareness) passes through the lens and is focused on the film. The light shining through the film is then projected on the screen, where the movie of your life is played out. Pure Eufeeling is becoming aware of Eufeeling just before light passes through the film. Any thoughts you have while aware of Pure Eufeeling become part of the movie film, written into the script if you will, and are projected onto the screen of life for all to see. This is the seat of miracles.

It is awareness at the Pure Eufeeling level that makes you the creator of your life. Or more accurately, you become the primal witness beyond the will of ego. Here, you are simultaneously the creator, the creation, and the unbounded awareness within and beyond both. It is from this level of awareness that you create miracles in your life. From Pure Eufeeling, you will quell the anxiety and frustration of financial difficulties, resolve the anger and mistrust in relationships, and open your eyes to your inner power that has been, until now, beleaguered by the rumble and rubble of your runaway mind. It is from this marvelous level of awareness that all life is renewed every instant of every day. Your life is no different.

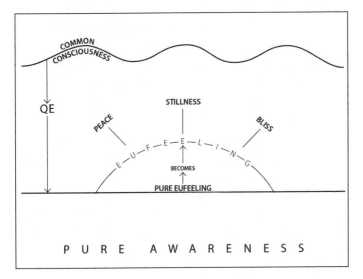

The Creator-Creation Paradox

When you experience Pure Eufeeling, you are at once the creator and beyond creation. I know, I know, it doesn't seem to make sense. Our minds function in the field of form and cannot comprehend the formless. Your mind will never wrap itself around this reality, but you can have a knowing, an intuition that goes beyond understanding. To your mind, it is a paradox. How can you be both unbounded awareness and bound by thoughts and things? Your mind tells the only story it knows. But remember, you are not your mind. You are pure awareness; the space between the thoughts that fills your mind. There is only one creation. However, when it is viewed through an individual body-mind, all of creation is narrowed down to the individual and is seen as *my* life. Pure Eufeeling raises you to your unbounded status of the observer-creator so that you can enjoy the best of both worlds.

This is a very important realization. What does observer-creator mean? It means that you can change your life, create it anew, and at the same time, not get caught in the often debilitating wash of emotions and desires that always accompany efforts to control our lives through common conscious. It means that you no longer have to create great effort to find success. It means that you are free to languish in the joy of being fully human. In just a few moments, you are going to learn QE Intention, the technology of effortless fulfillment. You will learn to be successful on every level of your life. And the beauty of QE Intention is that you do not need to understand a single thing we have just been talking about. Talking and thinking are mental functions relegated to our process-bound minds. QE Intention will still work wonders for you even if you don't have a clue to how it works. Fortunately, you don't have to take my word for it. It will work even if you don't believe in it. In a few short pages, you will prove it to yourself.

QE Intention is a reproducible, scientific process so simple that you can't fail. You will be in complete control when you become the silent witness, uninvolved in what you create. I know it sounds contradictory, but that doesn't matter. QE Intention will work for you regardless of what your mind thinks. You will have absolute control over your life as long as what you want to create will cause no harm. We all live under the universal influence of cause and effect, and trying to bend those laws in our favor never turns out to our complete benefit. When having a QE Intention, you, your loved ones, and the rest of the world are protected from wrong thinking and injurious action. When experiencing Pure Eufeeling, you can do no harm. If you want something that is supported by the laws of nature, you will get it. It is just that simple. But listen to this: If you want something that is not right for you, something greater will be offered in its place. When Mother Nature's children awaken from the ego-dreams of everyday living, she offers them her greatest gifts. She will oversee the unfolding of the laws of cause and effect on your behalf. When you do QE Intention, you may want a bicycle and end up with a BMW. All you need do is desire, sit back, and wait.

QE Intention will prepare you to receive without resistance what is offered. You will be guided to greater success than you anticipate when you let the natural flow of creation lead you. You will naturally let go of your attachment to a path or idea or object when it will create more trouble than it is worth. In other words, from your private position at the heart of creation, you will be the first one to know if something will work. You will be the first to hear the gentle urgings from the silent space beyond your mind. You will be the first to enjoy the fruits of your nonlabor, completely accepting what is, as it is.

QE Intention is the vital element in any intention work. The further away from Eufeeling one tries to create success, the harder one must work. Intention work should be effortless. This is especially true when we are manifesting our desires on the material plane. The further you are from the absolute organizing harmony of Pure Eufeeling, the more rules you will have to follow and the more detailed your intention must become. Traditional intention work can require a good bit of effort, detail, and repetition. If you want a new home, you may be asked to build it in your mind. You may be told to create it brick by brick, down to the color and position of every light switch, electrical outlet, and cabinet handle. This method infers that the more detailed you are, the more the image is burned into your mind and the better will be your chances of owning that new home. There may be many rules attached to your practice of intention. You might be asked to create your intention in a positive frame of mind. You may be asked to refer to the goal as if you have already achieved it. You may be encouraged to repeat your intention as often as you think about it.

These practices that entail repetition and minute detail are many times successful but rarely for the reason we think. We know it is the infinite organizing power of Pure Eufeeling that manifests our dreams and fulfills our deepest desires. When the mind is wrapped up in infinite detail or continuous repetition, it sometimes automatically slips into a deeper state of stillness within the mind. It does so despite the incessant activity around manifesting the intention. In this way, the intention becomes almost like a mantra, actively entraining the mind until it fatigues. If the mind is sufficiently rested, it will dip into some of the quieter levels of mind. There the seed will be planted and begin to grow toward fruition. If the mind is tired, it will wander off to seek more interesting subject matter to explore, or it will just fall asleep.

It depends how deeply the intention seed was planted in the quieter regions of your mind as to how quickly and completely you will see results. Some people are naturally more inclined to access these quiet levels and are able to plant their intention seeds deeper. These people are the ones whose intentions seem to work for them much of the time. If you are not able to quiet your mind, you can do exactly as those who are successful and still not see results. It can be very frustrating and raise doubts in your mind as to whether you are worthy of getting what you desire. This is not the case at all. It is not the intention, the process, or even the person that meets with failure. A successful intention relies on only one thing: the level of awareness. The deepest level of awareness we can experience is Pure Eufeeling. So, we could say that the effectiveness of your intention depends on the quality of your awareness. With little practice and less effort, everyone can learn to greatly improve the quality of their awareness and, therefore, the effectiveness of their intention work.

As you will soon find out, QE Intention requires no more effort than the slightest mental impulse to realize fruition of your greatest hopes and goals. You do not have to give up what you are doing right now. That's right, you can continue to do your intention work as you always have with one single, and I might add profound, addition. Instead of just thinking your intention or throwing in a little feeling to give it some emotional oomph, simply sink into the silent depths of your mind, the realm of infinite possibilities. You only have to add Pure Eufeeling to your intention work, and the improvement will be noticeable immediately.

One more thing before you learn how to have a QE Intention. Every intention has two parts to it: the object of the intention and the emotion that you attach to the intention. The object may be corporeal, like trees and keys and bumblebee's knees, or a car or a house. An object can also be less concrete, like higher education, a more compatible relationship, or greater spiritual harmony. The emotion attached to any intention usually springs out of a concern or fear that you will not get, or do not deserve, what you are asking for. For instance, you may apply for a new job that you really need. This is the object of your intention, and you may be very anxious about whether you will get it. In this case, your anxiety is the emotion attached to the intention. Your anxiety has grown out of a fear that you will not get the job. In many cases, if not most, the emotion can be more debilitating and cause more discomfort than not getting what you desire. Your worry about getting the job can interfere with actually getting the job. For instance, you can be the perfect candidate for the job but become so nervous you fail the interview, and the job goes to a less-qualified candidate.

The first thing that QE Intention does is to remove the emotional discord attached to achieving your goal. The quelling of the emotional disharmony does not take weeks or days or even hours. QE Intention immediately dissolves emotional discord so that all the creative energies can be focused on acquiring the goal. If eliminating emotional upset were the only thing you learned, it would be worth the price of this book a thousand times over. But there is more: much, much more.

Some systems of intention work actually encourage the addition of emotion to add momentum. Adding this kind of positive emotion to intention can have a stimulating effect. It can move us more quickly down the road to completion. But the emotion is the driving force not the guiding force.

That reminds me of the story of the man and his wife who were taking a long trip by car. They were heading south for the white sand beaches of Florida, and the man was taking an afternoon nap while his wife drove. He lazily woke from his slumber and felt the warm afternoon sun on the side of his face. He listened to the hum of the tires on the pavement and knew they were traveling at a very good speed. Then, all of a sudden, it dawned on him that the sun should be shining on the driver's side if they were traveling south. He sat up with a start and said, "We're heading north, the opposite direction we are supposed to be going!" "Yes," she replied with enthusiasm, "but we are making very good time." It does not matter how fast you travel if you are going in the wrong direction. Included in the QE intention traveler's kit is the perfect compass: Pure Eufeeling.

When you have a QE Intention, you cannot take yourself in the wrong direction, because you do nothing. You are just an observer, along for the ride. The QE Intention elicits a delicate impulse completely revealing what you want. How and when you get it is entirely up to the forces of creation. Eufeeling is the mastermind that organizes those forces on your behalf.

Let's say you are in a large city in a foreign country where you do not speak or read the language. You need to go all the way across town to reach your destination. You could rent a car and try to navigate the city on your own. But not knowing the local motor vehicle laws and unable to read your map or traffic signs, the chances of successfully reaching your destination without getting lost and discouraged are very slim. So you hire a taxi.

The driver knows how to best reach your destination. He knows how to avoid heavy traffic areas, construction sites, and detours, and he can show you points of interest along the way. At times during your trip, you may even be going in the opposite direction from where you want to go, but in the end, you will reach your destination more quickly, easily, and safely. As a passenger, the entire trip takes no effort on your part. You are the perfect observer, uninvolved in the actual technicalities of getting you to your destination. When you have a QE Intention, you give the driver (Eufeeling) your destination and then sit back and enjoy the ride.

When you have a QE Intention, you will not need to try and convince yourself of anything. Nor will you need to put energy into creating a positive atmosphere. It will all flow from you as naturally as water flows downhill. Actually, this is a good way to look at QE Intention. If you are a dewdrop on the tip of a leaf with the desire to merge with the unbounded ocean, you don't have to try to do anything to get there. Gravity draws you to the earth, where you merge with other drops and form a pool. Soon, the pool overflows, and you find yourself flowing toward the mother of all dewdrops: the ocean.

Will your journey be in a straight line? Never! At first, you would flow and pool and then flow and pool some more. While you are sitting around in the pool, you may feel that you are getting nowhere. But more and more drops are gathering behind you, and soon your collective momentum causes the pool to overflow and you find yourself again whooshing toward the great ocean. Sometimes you will flow to the right and to the left and even away from the ocean. Again, you may feel that you are wasting time, and you will never reach your goal at your present rate of progress. There is a saying in spiritual circles, "The closer the goal, the faster and easier the ride." You soon find yourself joining streams and rivers, and your ride toward union with the ocean truly is faster and easier. Gravity and the forces of fluid dynamics have guided you from leaf tip to ocean without any effort on your part. Worry and individual effort had little effect on the outcome. And so it is with QE Intention. Your delicate desire is enough to place you in the flow of the forces of creation, not to help you in your effort, but to carry you beyond effort to the successful realization of your desire. You become the witness to your own creation, the progenitor of peace and harmony, with nothing more than a single thought.

Main Points for Chapter 12

- Pure Eufeeling is awareness of pure awareness and Eufeeling simultaneously, before you perceive feelings like joy, peace, or bliss in your mind.

- People who can create miracles and materialize things out of thin air do so from the level of Pure Eufeeling.

- The more established one's awareness is in Pure Eufeeling, the more order is reflected in their lives.

- QE Intention works even if you don't understand or believe in it.

- If you want something that is supported by the laws of nature, you will get it. If you desire something that is not right for you, then you will be offered something greater in its place.

- Eufeeling is the vital element in any intention work.

- Intention work should be effortless.

- The further away from Eufeeling one tries to create success, the harder one must work.

- A successful intention relies on only one thing: your level of awareness.

- When you have a QE Intention, you give the driver (Eufeeling) your destination and then sit back and enjoy the ride.

༄

CHAPTER 13

How to Have a QE Intention

"Crave for a thing, you will get it. Renounce the craving, the object will follow you by itself."

— SWAMI SIVANANDA

An Intimate Celebration of Self

In a very short time, we have learned a great deal. We have had a number of enlightening experiences, learned a lot of neat things—not the least of which was QE and how to slip beneath the roiling waters of the fettered mind and find inner peace, the foundation for fulfillment. What we are about to learn is an ancient technology, dating back thousands years. It was a more intimate part of our lives then before our minds were enticed outward beyond necessity to play in the field of excess. Initially, we had to control our environment for our own survival. But in our exuberance, we endeavored to dominate her. In the process, we lost our Selves. The procedure you are about to learn is a technology from a far more simple time, when we were more at home with our Self. It is a simple and yet an ultimately prevailing technology, which will return to us that which we lost out of ignorance and inattentiveness. We have discussed a lot in preparation for this time, but in the end, QE Intention is a personal and intimate celebration of your Self. Its magic will still enfold you even if you understand nothing of what we have discussed. So, lay down your analytical tools if you like, and prepare to return to the primal state, before it was imposed upon by the mayhem of the modern mind.

A QE Intention session is a specific well-defined event, at least in the beginning. In time, your QE intention session will start and finish in the blink of an eye. It will require no preparation. But for now, we will go through the process step by step, ensuring that it becomes second nature for you. In a very short time, having a QE Intention will be as natural as thinking.

Now, please pay special attention to the following, as it is crucial to the successful execution of QE Intention. QE Intention is not arrived at like a traditional intention. The QE Intention itself is a singular thing, uncomplicated and straightforward. If you want a new house, you don't have to build it stick by stick or picture it vividly in your imagination. All you need is what is already waiting for you in your mind: your desire, the impression of your house that has already been formed. The desire for it was there even before you became aware of it. QE Intention is becoming aware of that already created desire in a special way so that the forces of creation want you to have it. QE Intention properly positions your desire so that it becomes a part of and supports a greater plan.

All your desires remain with you on some level until they are fulfilled. Most of the time, you will find them patiently settled in the quieter levels of your mind, waiting to be acknowledged. So, how do you acknowledge your desire-intention? Just become aware of it! But remember, the success of your intention depends on the quality of your awareness. Pure Eufeeling is the most refined experience of awareness we can have. When you become aware of your desire-intention while aware of Pure Eufeeling, it has the greatest potential for fulfillment on every level of your life.

When you do QE Intention, you form a partnership, as it were, with pure awareness. Pure awareness is the foundation for all creation. As pure awareness is projected through Eufeeling, it creates what you recognize as your life. Eufeeling, the purest expression of pure awareness, knows what it is doing. It is best to let it build your house for you. QE Intention deftly and delicately places your desire-intention in the most subtle expression of Eufeeling, at the very seat of creation.

Do Nothing—Gain Everything

The ideal house for you may not be the one you have in your mind. Most of the time, an innocent desire from the very quiet level of your mind gets buffeted and pushed about by your more bullish, less-orderly thoughts. Eufeeling knows what is right for you better than you do. And it knows how to give it to you in the most efficient way, without creating disharmony to yourself or others. If the house you have in your mind is right for you, you will get it exactly as you see it. More than likely, though, there is a much better house for you than you have imagined. Your nonspecific intention will give Eufeeling free reign to rally all the forces of creation around, finding your perfect domicile. The more specific you are, and the more willpower you impose on your intention, the more you distort the innocence of your original desire and the less likely you are to fulfill that desire. You may work very hard and get your house exactly as you see it in your mind but still not feel completely satisfied. Maybe you know someone who got exactly what they planned but couldn't enjoy it, because it wasn't what they needed. During the QE Intention process, when I ask you to become aware of your intention, just have a faint and easy idea of what you want. Then let Eufeeling do all the heavy lifting. Okay, ready to do nothing and get everything?

First, become aware of what you want. Easily let your thoughts shift to the desire-intention that your mind has already created. Don't try to change it into something else. It is already perfect. Your desire has been created from you. In all creation, there is not another like it. Acknowledge your desire and accept it just as it is. Trying to make it into something better or more tangible will only change it into something less perfect. So, when I ask you to think of your intention, all you have to do is become aware of what is already there. Simple enough, yes?

Experience: How to Have a QE Intention

Find a comfortable place to sit where you won't be disturbed for about 15 minutes. Settle in, and begin the QE process just as you learned earlier in this book, only stay seated with your eyes closed. Begin by watching your thoughts without effort or expectation. Soon, as before, your thoughts will slow and become quieter or disappear altogether. Anywhere along the way, you may become aware of Eufeeling: a feeling of quietness, lightness, gentleness, peace, or some other good feeling. Because of your practice over the last few days, you may find Eufeeling waiting for you as soon as you close your eyes. Wherever you find Eufeeling, allow your awareness to clearly and gently be with it. Allow the impulse of awareness to easily embrace the tender reflection of Eufeeling.

Continue your awareness of Eufeeling in this easy way for a full five minutes, or if you feel very quiet or still in mind and body, or you have periods where you are unaware of your mind and body. (Be careful not to look ahead or anticipate these changes in body and mind. The increased mental activity of looking for them can keep them from occurring. The proper approach here is to just check and see if you have been unaware of body and mind or are feeling very quiet or still.)

Become aware of your Eufeeling. Identify it. Is it peace or lightness or bliss or joy? Just easily pay attention to what it is . . . watch it like a cat watching a mouse hole. Watch with eager attention to see what it will do next.

As you watch your Eufeeling in this quiet state, note that you feel some stillness. Now, become more clearly aware of this stillness. Observe this stillness with quiet attention. Note that while observing stillness, nothing is moving . . . that includes your mind. Everything is still, not moving. This is Pure Eufeeling.

You know you are aware, but there is nothing to be aware of. Your body, your mind, all of creation is still as if holding its breath.

Now you are ready to plant your intention in the fertile soil of Pure Eufeeling. Settled deeply within the stillness of Pure Eufeeling, let your mind easily shift over to your desire. However it manifests in your mind, become aware of what it is that you want. Then, just as easily, have a gentle thought of your intention, what it will be like when that desire is fulfilled. This is just a flicker of a thought without any detail whatsoever. Don't try to build or create an intention. Only observe it in its most simple but complete state, innocent and pure. Maintain your role solely as observer.

Let your awareness return to the stillness of Pure Eufeeling. If Pure Eufeeling is not there, some aspect of Eufeeling, peace, joy, lightness, love, will be. Within that good feeling, you will always find stillness. Stillness is in everything. Observe the stillness as before, until all movement stops. When you are once again aware of Pure Eufeeling, you have completed your QE Intention.

You can repeat this as many times as you like each session. Follow each perception of stillness with an easy awareness of your desire-intention and then return to stillness.

That is all there is to QE Intention. If your desire is motivated by a negative emotion, like anxiety or guilt, you will find that you are already feeling better. That is the first of the fixing. But you have also started the wheels of creation in motion to bring you fulfillment on the material level. Just sit back and watch as the genius of life opens opportunity after opportunity for you to enjoy.

Let's go back and take a closer look at the actual mechanics of your QE Intention. The first element of QE Intention I want to pay particular attention to is Pure Eufeeling. It is the subtlest and most powerful awareness and, therefore, the most abstract. While QE Intention works best from awareness of Pure Eufeeling, it also works extremely well when you are aware of the less-abstract feelings that are associated with Eufeeling. By that I mean the quietness, lightness, peace, joy, or bliss you feel when you are aware of Eufeeling. (Don't forget, the feelings of love and peace of Eufeeling come out of the stillness of Pure Eufeeling. They are the first activity in your mind after the nonactivity of Pure Eufeeling.)

Here's my point. When you first begin doing QE Intention, you may not quite distinguish between the stillness of Pure Eufeeling and the peace or love of the more common Eufeeling. In fact, if you are searching for it, you may miss it. Searching is an activity and directly opposite to the innocent and simple observation of the nonactivity of stillness. I know, I know, it's peculiar, but I didn't make the rules; I'm just here to point them out for you. The good news is that QE Intention works with either Eufeeling or Pure Eufeeling. I taught you QE Intention from the most refined perspective of Pure Eufeeling so that you know it exists. But you can just as easily, and with almost the same results, have a QE Intention by becoming aware of whichever feeling Eufeeling is generating in your mind. So, your QE Intention might go something like this:

- Become easily aware of your Eufeeling (quietness, peace, lightness, love, and so on).

- Easily let your awareness fall on your desire-intention, and quietly watch to see what happens.

- Gently return to the stillness of Pure Eufeeling.

For the sake of ease and to eliminate confusion, from this point on I will use the word *Eufeeling* to stand for both Pure Eufeeling and Eufeeling (with feeling). Then you will know that Pure Eufeeling is included every time I just use the word *Eufeeling*. However, in your practice of QE Intention, you will continue to look for Pure Eufeeling. Deal? Good, let's move on.

Let us spend a minute or two on intention. The QE Intention includes both the desire and the intention to fulfill that desire. When having a QE Intention, you can be consciously aware of both the desire and the intention, or you may find your awareness just falling on one without the other. While doing your QE Intention, you may only become aware of your desire or only your intention. In actuality, they come from a single source, and awareness of either one will satisfy both. Either is just right as long as you do not try to manipulate what reflects on the screen of your mind. Just have the impulse to become aware of your intention and then whatever appears is just right. Again, for the sake of simplicity, from now on I will just use the word *intention* to mean both the desire and the intention that goes hand in hand with it.

Of Puppies and Dandelion Puffs

Here is a simple way to have a QE Intention and have fun doing it. It has its own charm and is inherently as powerful as what I have described previously. I prefer this alternative method myself and use it almost exclusively. Here's how it goes.

After I have become aware of Eufeeling and have just become aware of my desire, I have a delicate thought that depicts the fulfillment of my desire in a fun and uplifting way. For instance, if my desire is to have a happier relationship with another person, I might have the thought *happiness of children at play* or *flowing as effortlessly as a river.* Then I would let my mind return to Eufeeling. Eufeeling will know exactly what to do with your QE Intention form. After all, it gave you the image to begin with. Now that you are conscious of your intention image, Eufeeling will start the wheels of creation in motion.

Many people prefer this method, as it tends to add an element of lightness and play mirroring more closely the actual joy of creation. You can use any phrase that comes to your mind that reflects the spirit of your intention. Just keep your intention image to a single word or a short phrase, and have it show action. I'll give you some examples of forming intentions I have used below. While you can use my intentions, it's better to eventually allow your own to surface in your consciousness. And keep in mind these intentions can change between QE Intention sessions or even during them. Don't be rigid. Whatever pops into your mind and supports the fulfillment of your desire is just perfect. Here are a few of my examples:

Eufeeling!

Relationships

- Compassion of a mother
- Friendly as a dog
- Open like the sky
- Mysterious as the ocean

Finances

- Love as money
- Watering my money tree
- Giving from a bottomless well
- Money from my fingertips

Health

- Solid as a mountain
- Light as dandelion fuzz
- Clear as morning sunlight
- Flowing like the wind

Spiritual

- Still as a stone
- Knowing without knowing
- All things are my essence (Eufeeling)
- Light without flame

Making an Intention Sandwich

At times, you may find your intention changing. If so, let it change the way it wants. It may seem to be going in a different direction than you consciously want, but don't interfere. Let your intention express itself. What is happening at this point is that *you* are reinventing yourself. This is the rearrangement of the iron filings as the magnet (Eufeeling) lines up the chaotic elements of your life into perfect order. At this point, you are open to all possible solutions from every direction of creation. This is not the case when you have an intention in common consciousness, where control and imagination are not completely pure but subservient to either distorting emotions, inflexible logic, or both.

You see, you have your intention lovingly nestled between slices of Eufeeling. You are creating something very special here. You could look at it as if you were making an intention sandwich. If Eufeeling were the bread, you would be laying one slice on the table of pure awareness. That slice lies *still* on the table. On that still slice of bread, you lovingly place your intention meat (or soy burger for our vegan and vegetarian readers). Then place another slice of Eufeeling bread over your intention, and voilà, the perfect intention sandwich! Of course, I'm having a little fun with you, but this illustration makes the point that QE Intention is made in this way: Eufeeling-intention-Eufeeling.

Or another way of looking at QE Intention is through the eyes of universal Love. Universal Love is like your mother. She wants you to have everything you desire. She doesn't see your desire as something separate from you. She loves your desire as she loves you. When you have a QE Intention, universal Love embraces it in her Eufeeling arms. She nurtures it, loves it, and encourages it to grow and prosper. If like a child you desire something that is harmful or wasteful, she will lead you in a different, more productive direction. She might even distract you with a greater gift that will quell your original desire and leave you with much, much more.

When you have a QE Intention and gently lay your intention on the silent bed of Eufeeling, it can do one of two things. It may immediately fade back into Eufeeling, or it may begin to take on a life of its own, like a movie. If so, watch as your intention movie plays on the screen of your awareness for a minute or so. Then allow your awareness to easily shift back to Eufeeling. If your intention dissolved back into Eufeeling right away, after a minute or so of stillness, awareness will have the impulse to return to your intention.

So, your intention either dissolves back into Eufeeling or it unfolds in your mind like a movie. Either experience is perfect. In either case, when you again become aware of Eufeeling, make sure you become very clearly aware of it. In that stillness, watch Eufeeling like a cat watching a mouse hole to see what will happen. After a minute or so with Eufeeling, again easily become aware of your intention. Continue this process of alternating between Eufeeling and your intention. Gently repeat the cycle as many times as you like and as feels comfortable. This is how to have a QE Intention. Now, finish the QE Intention session with two to five minutes, or longer if you like, of QE. That is, being aware of Eufeeling whenever it is there and letting everything else go its separate way.

In essence, you are thinking your intention and then letting it swim free in the fertile waters of Eufeeling. You do not want to hold on to your intention in any way. Only let the impulse of your intention slip into your awareness, recognize it, and then let it dissolve back into the fullness of Eufeeling.

As I mentioned previously, it may be that instead of dissolving back into Eufeeling, your intention begins to unfold its hidden parts like the petals of a blossoming flower. This is an automatic unfolding, not something you initiate. Just watch like a movie playing on the screen of your mind. Do not interfere with this unfolding in any way. The universal creative forces are reorganizing time and events in your favor. This is how your life story gets rewritten. Your intention-movie may or may not make sense to you as it unfolds before you. No matter what plays out at this time, do not get involved. Only observe and enjoy. If you get wrapped up in your intention-movie and forget to return to Eufeeling for a couple of minutes, no problem. Just quietly return to Eufeeling when that sequence of thoughts fades out. On a similar note, your mind may begin to wonder to unrelated topics. No problem here either. When you realize your mind is meandering, have a quiet impulse to return to pure Eufeeling and make another intention sandwich.

Many times while having a QE Intention, desires related to other parts of your life might show up. With QE Intention, you can often kill two, three, or more birds with one stone. All your desires are related to each other, and all of them spring from the ego's basic desire to be reunited with Eufeeling. If other desires present themselves to you during a QE Intention session, it's okay to enjoy them as a substitute for your original intention.

When you start a brand-new QE Intention session, however, always start with your original intention.

At times of great emotional stress, you may find that your QE Intention session is filled with thoughts. This might be less enjoyable than at other times, but many thoughts are not a problem. Don't fight the thoughts thinking that you shouldn't be having them. If they're there, then that's exactly what you should be having. When you realize your mind is off topic, just begin to watch the thoughts attentively without trying to interfere, just like when you learned the QE process. During these sessions, you probably won't experience the deep stillness of Pure Eufeeling. That's just fine. When the relative periods of quiet present themselves, become aware of your intention and then Eufeeling to whatever degree is open to you. Each QE Intention session will be different. Don't try to make them the same or make them different. Accept what is there just as it is. QE Intention will work for you no matter what your subjective experience.

For the most astonishing results, have several QE Intention sessions a day. I recommend your sessions last between five and ten minutes each at first. Besides mobilizing the creative forces of creation to fulfill your desires, there are many other benefits to a QE Intention session. In a very short time, you'll be able to have a QE Intention between heartbeats, anywhere, anytime. But don't get in a hurry. This is not a goal to shoot for but something that will unfold naturally in its own time.

You can have QE Intention for any kind of a desire. It doesn't always have to be serious or important. Do QE Intention all day long. Have a QE Intention for the most frivolous of desires, like a hot fudge sundae or a new pair of nose tweezers. Go ahead, have a ball . . . you've earned it.

In the next few chapters, while you and QE Intention become good buddies, I will help you realize the power of the process you have just learned. I would like to go into more detail on how to apply QE Intention with such concerns as chronic illness, financial concerns, emotional management, and solving problems. I will also add techniques on how to help others over the hurdles to realizing their deepest desires. Before going on to the next chapter, preferably immediately, I would like you to do another full QE Intention session. Go ahead, put the book in your lap, and let one of your desires drift to the surface of your consciousness. Gently become aware of Eufeeling . . . your intention . . . Eufeeling . . . and enjoy a full, blissful QE Intention session.

(*Note:* Even if you are not experiencing any emotional discord, I recommend reading the next chapter on emotional management, because it contains basic instructions that can be applied to the remaining chapters. This will save you from having to read the same material in each chapter.)

Main Points for Chapter 13

- QE Intention is an ancient technology dating back thousands of years.

- QE Intention begins by becoming aware of the deep stillness of Pure Eufeeling.

- Then become quietly aware of the desire-intention your mind has already created.

- QE Intention is like an intention sandwich, with your intention between two slices of Eufeeling stillness.

- The intention movie on the screen of your mind is Eufeeling rewriting your life to fulfill your desire.

- For the most astonishing results, have several QE Intention sessions a day.

- Enjoy all kinds of desires: serious, fun, or frivolous.

CHAPTER 14

Emotional Management

*"Giving space to others—and to yourself—is vital.
Love cannot flourish without it."*

— Eckhart Tolle

Even the Dalai Lama Gets Angry

I don't think we really have to build a case for positive emotional health. I do not know a single individual who is beyond the touch of emotional discord. Even the Dalai Lama says he gets angry from time to time. At one time or another, all of us wrestle with negative emotions. All too often, all too many of us are overwhelmed to the point that our lives are negatively impacted.

The problem with runaway emotions is that they trample all over our logical faculties. Emotions bend and distort our ability to think clearly and tangibly. Often, the person who is swayed by negative emotions isn't even aware that they have a problem. When approached by a well-meaning friend who points out their emotional aberrancy, the afflicted may look at them as if they just beamed down from a planet devoid of intelligent life. They simply can't believe that they have a problem, much less that they are the problem.

It does not matter whether you think you are the problem or someone else is, QE Intention will work beautifully. It works equally as well for the well-meaning friend as it does for the person who is emotionally distraught. That is because you can do QE Intention for yourself or for another. That's right; you can have a QE Intention for another person's welfare and feel completely confident that only good will be done. No, you do not need their permission to have a QE Intention for them. That is because you are not *doing* anything. As you already know, once you have a QE Intention, you are done. Your intention is nestled in the nurturing arms of Eufeeling and will be worked out through Eufeeling's design, not yours.

Now, I think this is obvious but it needs to be said. I am not trained in the psychological arts, and I do not feel that QE or QE Intention should be substituted for professional psychological care. Professionals in the field of clinical psychology are using QE and QE Intention to help their patients overcome acute psychological trauma as well as chronic concerns. Many of these professionals are excited to find that these Eufeeling technologies rapidly reduce the suffering of their patients. It is my hope that in the near future, we will be able to sponsor clinical studies as to the efficacy of QE in the field of psychology. In the meantime, know that for the layperson, QE and QE Intention are extremely valuable in reducing and eliminating psychological discord, but they should never be substituted for the care of a licensed professional. Of course, this statement applies to all physical concerns in every field of health care. Now, let us return to our regularly scheduled programming.

We have already talked about how an intention has two parts: the object and the emotion that gets attached to that object. When we have a QE Intention for emotional discord, the object may necessarily be the emotion. Or you may experience the more traditional bifurcation into object and emotion. If your mother-in-law came to visit for a long weekend and is still telling your wife six months later what a big mistake she made marrying you, you have the object (your mother-in-law) and the emotions attached to it. The emotion could be anger, frustration, anxiety, confusion, depression, angst, uncontrollable sorrow, or inconsolable grief. And because it involves your mother-in-law, it's probably all of them together.

I separated intention into two parts mostly for the sake of illustration. You do not have to be concerned with these two aspects of intention unless you care to. QE Intention takes care of the whole ball of wax at one time, without you having to do anything. That said, many people like to play with the parts of their intention while they are wrapped in the blanket of bliss we know as Eufeeling. This is completely a matter of preference. As long as you are aware of Eufeeling, your intention will be fulfilled as fully as the laws of nature will allow.

Experience: QE Intention for Emotions

I recommend that for the first several sessions of emotional QE Intention, you work with problems of a minor to moderate intensity. Once you feel comfortable and gain a little experience with the QE Intention process, you can move on to more demanding emotional concerns.

Sit quietly, where you will not be disturbed for five to ten minutes. With eyes closed, allow your mind to become aware of what is bothering you. Bring up the situation and the emotions that go with it. Let it get as strong as it will and then grade it on a scale from 0 to 10, 10 being absolutely unbearable and 0 being free of discomfort. Remember your starting number, as you will repeat this test when you are done with this session.

Do QE for two to three minutes, becoming aware of Eufeeling. You should feel some quietness in your mind and relaxation in your body. Let your mind go to the problem and then right away to the solution, how you would like to resolve the problem. These two steps, becoming aware of the problem and then solution, is a fairly fluid process. You think of one then the other, and then let them both go as your awareness returns to Eufeeling. (Remember, Eufeeling means the nothing of Pure Eufeeling or the feelings of simple Eufeeling. Either is fine.)

If you were having the problem with your mother-in-law cited previously, it might go something like this: From the easy fullness of Eufeeling, your mind becomes aware of the emotions you experience with your mother-in-law and the situation you have surrounding these emotions. You don't have to direct your mind in any way, because you will find it drawn to the most troubling aspect all on its own. You only spend enough time on the emotions and situation to recognize it. That will happen in the time it takes you to have one or two thoughts. Then, just as easily, let your awareness go to the solution. Again, this is an automatic process, so give your mind free reign.

At this point, you might see your mother-in-law picking up her bags, giving you a great big hug, and boarding the plane to Seattle to take up residence in your sister-in-law's house. Your solution almost always presents itself without any conscious effort on your part. If it's a little stubborn, you can prime the process by lightly thinking of a solution and letting that settle into Eufeeling. QE Intention is always fun and uplifting. Don't make it a chore, even when the subject matter is quite serious. Remember, you don't have to build your house stick by stick. Just a gentle nudge is all Eufeeling needs.

Have your QE Intention every minute or so for three to five minutes, and end your session with three to five minutes of QE or just being aware of Eufeeling. Make sure you don't jump right up and launch yourself into activity. Take a little time; let your mind wander for a while as you prepare for the day that awaits you. While you are taking this time, revisit the emotions and situation just as you did at the start of your QE Intention session. Let the emotions get as strong as they will, and again, grade them from 0 to 10. In almost every case, you will find that your emotions, anxiety, fear, anger, sorrow, grief, guilt, or frustration will have dropped remarkably.

Now, and this is very important, forget about what you have just done, and go about your daily routine as if nothing has happened. Although a great deal has already happened, most of it is going on behind the scenes. Leave it there. Let the organizing forces of creation do their job, while you go about the businesses of living just as you always have. Believe me, your life will change immeasurably by what you have just done, or actually have just not done. If you keep checking your life to see if your intention is working, you can actually hinder the process to a slight degree. Each time you check to see if progress has been made, you slightly recalibrate your intention from your present level of common consciousness. While you can never completely overshadow a single session of QE Intention, you can slow it a bit. Fortunately, any distortions you might introduce will be neutralized by your next QE Intention session. So, do your QE Intention session and go about your life as usual. When your gift arrives, you will be surprised, not to mention grateful, and just a little awestruck. You did it without doing anything. It doesn't get any better than that.

Mist on the Water

In some systems of intention work, and energy healing as well, creating waves of harmony is likened to dropping a pebble in a quiet pond. At the point at which the pebble, the traditional intention, drops into the pond, waves move outward in concentric circles. The energy waves then return to you, the point at which the pebble disturbed the pond, bringing with them information on how to be successful in your world. Having a QE Intention is more like allowing an ethereal mist to settle ever so lightly on the still waters of Pure Eufeeling. We do not want to disturb those waters but allow them to remain a clear reflection of creation. We do not want to endeavor to impose our limited will on creation. Even to think so is folly and only fosters the illusion of control, which quickly leads to stronger desires and ultimately increased suffering. Rather, from our silent vantage point on the surface of the still pond of Pure Eufeeling, we tenderly open our awareness to our QE Intention and then watch as it gently kisses the surface of Pure Eufeeling. This is the magical moment, the flawless conception, when all of creation awakens to your desire.

Your work is done. On the most precious level of life, your desire has already been fulfilled. Your disruptive desires and unsettling emotions have dissipated like a cool mist in warm sunlight. Now, with a sense of playful expectancy, you need only wait to see in what wrapping your present will arrive.

Main Points for Chapter 14

- At one time or another, all of us wrestle with negative emotions.

- Emotions bend and distort our ability to think clearly and tangibly.

- You can have a QE Intention for another's emotional well-being.

- Once you are finished having a QE Intention, go about your life as usual with no expectations.

- QE Intention is like allowing an ethereal mist to settle on the still waters of Pure Eufeeling. We do not want to disturb those waters but allow them to remain a clear reflection of creation.

CHAPTER 15

Chronic Illness

"Suffering is a sign that you are out of touch with the truth. If you are suffering you are asleep. Do you want a sign that you are asleep? Here it is: You're suffering."

— ANTHONY DE MELLO

Eufeeling Heals

Chronic illnesses are long-lasting, involve prolonged care, and have a fairly low percentage cure rate. As our bodies and minds age, our ability to spontaneously repair damaged tissues diminishes. Old age sees a greater share of chronic illnesses, and a lower percentage of these cases are cured. Although chronic illnesses are certainly not restricted to our older population, that is where you will find a plethora of these conditions, including arthritis, heart disease, diabetes, and the most commonly feared cancer. The death rate from chronic illnesses is high even among younger sufferers. Chronic illness creates a sizable burden on family members, the community, and even entire countries. Obviously, the greatest burden is carried by the individual who has such a disease, and it is the individual sufferer who will benefit most from QE Intention.

If you do not have a chronic illness but you would like to help someone who does, QE Intention is tailor-made for you. Here's how to go about helping a chronically suffering friend, family member, or even a perfect stranger by having a QE Intention.

Experience: QE Intention for Helping Others with Chronic Illness

Do QE for three to five minutes, or until you feel quite settled in Eufeeling. Become aware of the individual (your partner) and how their illness is affecting them. Do this as if you were watching them from across the room, as a simple observer of their outward condition. If you begin to feel a little emotional, don't worry. Your personal involvement will not diminish the effectiveness of your QE Intention for them, and it will also be considerably healing for you. Don't try to feel the emotion or to push it out. If you become emotionally involved, acknowledge that you are, and continue with your awareness of your partner's symptoms. You only need to spend from a few seconds to 10 or 15 seconds and then let everything dissolve into Eufeeling. Remember to become clearly and attentively aware of Eufeeling. Enjoy the easy feeling of Eufeeling for a minute or so.

Now, have a simple thought of your partner. Picture them as before, with their symptoms. This time, become aware that their body, mind, and emotions are filled with the bliss of Eufeeling. Recognize that their every thought and emotion is submerged in the beauty of Eufeeling. Become aware that every atom of every molecule of every cell in their body is alive with the harmony and healing influence of Eufeeling. Innocently observe your mental movie to see how they react. Do this for a minute or so and then return to Eufeeling. Repeat this three-phase process one or two more times, observing their symptoms, becoming aware of Eufeeling, watching how they respond to being filled with Eufeeling, and back to Eufeeling. Finish your QE Intention session with three to five minutes of QE.

The power and speed at which QE Intention works for chronic sufferers is nothing short of amazing. QE Intention always has an immediate effect. How quickly you will see results in their symptomatology depends on the type and severity of illness and the sufferer's constitution. If you are able to get objective feedback like blood-sugar levels and blood pressure readings, you will see improvement right away. Also, consider having your partner do the pre- and posttest for both physical and emotional discomfort. In most cases, you will see immediate, and many times drastic, results.

Stick precisely to the simple formula described above. Ego plays no part in QE Intention. Do not envision your partner as healing or as being healed. This will not help in their recovery. You are not the healer. QE Intention is not the healer. Healing will come from the creative forces that issue forth from the wisdom and compassion inherent in Eufeeling. Whether our partners are cured or not is really not up to us. We can have the desire and the intention for our partner to heal, and this is as it should be. But the infinite number of possibilities in which the disease process can be expressed is beyond the comprehension of our limited minds. Better we respect the unfolding of the forces of nature as beyond our control. Do QE Intention and then enjoy being present with your partner, or just go on with your life business as usual. When it is time, Mother Nature will tap you on the shoulder and let you have a look at her handiwork.

You Can't Manufacture Nonattachment

Having a QE Intention for a chronic illness that is manifesting in your body-mind needs a slightly different orientation than when we do this work for someone else. As you might suspect, when you work on yourself, you have a vested interest in the outcome and, therefore, tend to be more attached to the results. This attachment is fear motivated, so it is filtered through your ego. Consequently, effectiveness is diminished significantly. So, the trick with self–QE Intention is nonattachment.

You cannot manufacture nonattachment. You cannot try to be unattached to your illness or anything else for that matter. Trying means effort toward a goal. A goal means that there is a path involved. It says that where you are is not good enough, and you want to be somewhere better. This means that you want to change what is. If life is perfect just as it is, wanting to change it means that you deny the perception of present perfection.

I can just hear you thinking with some measure of incredulity, *Of course I don't want to be where I am. I'm chronically ill. I want to be free of my illness.* This is obvious when you are ill. Where you are is not where you want to be, and you strive to reach your goal of being free of your disease. But that is just the point I want to make. It is a subtle and, therefore, potent shift in perception that can make all the difference between living life in fullness or in suffering, regardless of whether or not you have a life-threatening disease.

When you have a chronic illness, the main issue is not really the disease but your perception of it. If you own your body and your mind, when it is threatened in any way, your very essence is threatened. Ego thinks the body-mind is his, and he spends huge amounts of energy trying to protect it. Ego feels that if the body-mind dies, it, too, will die. QE Awareness transcends ego awareness and knows that destruction of the body-mind does not lead to destruction of Self. As we have already discussed, the essence of Self is timeless and beyond destruction.

I don't mean to sound offhanded, but bodies come and go. It is often said by those who have suffered deeply that there are worse things than death. The worst thing you can do to life is attach to death. As soon as your body is born, it begins dying. Attachment to your body is attachment to death. No matter how hard ego tries to keep things together, in the end, your temple will collapse. There are a lot of things that illness can teach us. But ultimately, there is only one lesson worth learning: We are not our body-mind. We are unbounded grace and joy and love all wrapped up in the celestial shell of Eufeeling. What good is it to beat a disease but lose your soul in the process? One thing is guaranteed: as you age, illness and infirmity will follow. Yes, you can cheat death a little here and there, but in the end, the house always wins.

Probably more than anywhere else on this Earth, the culture here in the United States is exceptionally youth oriented. We have what I feel is an unhealthy attitude toward aging, dying, and death. We Americans work very hard to put off thinking about the end of our lives. In many cultures, the aged are revered for their wisdom. They are protected and cared for in their old age and live with their family until they die. This is not so in my country.

We are fanatical about maintaining a youthful appearance and will go to drastic measures to appear younger than we are. Just a few decades ago, cosmetic surgery was a rarity. Today, such surgery is much more common, even in children barely into their teens. Yes, we should take care of our bodies and minds through the appropriate mental and physical exercise, nutrition, ample "alone time," and wholesome social interaction. No, we shouldn't use these activities as a club to beat off the perceived snakes of aging, dying, and death. Neither denying the fear nor attacking it will work to give us the inner peace we so desperately seek. For that we already have everything we need. When we have a QE Intention, we forfeit the field of death in favor of the joy of living beyond bounds.

Experience: QE Intention for Your Chronic Illness (The QE Body-Emotion Scan)

Start by sitting comfortably with your eyes closed, and do QE for three to five minutes, or until the quiet, stillness of Eufeeling is with you. Now, become aware of any discomfort or symptoms that you have, even if you do not attribute them to your illness. Let your awareness easily scan your body. As you become aware of each indication of illness in your body, let your awareness linger there for a few seconds before moving to the next symptom. When you have finished scanning your body in this way, and this should take no more than a minute or two, have the impulse to return to Eufeeling.

After a minute or so of being aware of Eufeeling, have the thought to return to your body. Again, pay attention to the different regions of your body and the symptoms that appear there. Note that these symptoms may have moved or may have increased or decreased in intensity; you may even become aware of new symptoms that did not appear the first time. This is an indication that healing is already taking place. Regardless of what or where the symptom is, when you become aware of it this time, look to see if there is an emotion attached to that symptom. If you find an emotion attached to the symptom, easily observe it for several seconds and then move on to the next symptom. Both the body scan and the emotional scan should last no more than a minute or two each. Now, return to the stillness and peace of Eufeeling for about a minute.

Again, easily allow your awareness to fall on your body-mind, including the attached emotions. Become aware of your body, your symptoms, and your emotions at the same time you are aware of Eufeeling. Recognize that every thought, sensation, and emotion is submerged in Eufeeling. Your symptom and emotion are there at the same time Eufeeling is there. Notice that every atom of every molecule of every cell in your body is alive with the harmony

*and healing influence of Eufeeling. Give it no direc-
tion. Resist the urge to direct energy to a specific area
of illness or discomfort. This will be done by Eufeeling far more effectively and quickly than by limited
you. Enjoy doing nothing and being everything for a
minute or two, and return to the welcoming arms of
Eufeeling for a minute or so. Repeat this three-phase
process three or more times as you like. Remember to
separate each phase—the body scan, the emotional
scan and the realization of Eufeeling, and all three
simultaneously—with a minute or so of awareness
of Pure Eufeeling. Finish your QE Intention session
with three to five minutes of QE.*

If you are bedridden, you may want to rest for a longer period with eyes closed, or even take a nap. When
you are ill, you can do QE and QE Intention as often as
you like. Although neither QE nor QE Intention are healing techniques, Eufeeling generates a huge and harmonious healing energy that will flood your body-mind,
allowing it to heal much, much more quickly.

You may have noticed that at no time during the QE
Intention do we direct energy. Nor do we imagine healing taking place or in any way interject control into the
process. You are only encouraged to move your awareness from one perception of relative reality to another.
So, the only exertion involved in QE Intention is the
almost effortless impulse to become aware. Herein lies
the secret to the power and remarkable effectiveness of
QE Intention.

Jeffrey's Story

As I write you, I have a good friend who is recovering from cancer. He is in his early 50s; has a healthy, active lifestyle; and is a very loving individual. One day while he and a friend were sailing on a lake in the Austrian Alps, he began to experience what he described as, "flu-like symptoms." The symptoms quickly worsened, and Jeffrey was taken to a local hospital. They ran tests on him, and the next day, he found out that he had a four-inch malignant tumor in his lungs, the result of a very aggressive, stage 4 lymphoma. He was strongly urged to return to the United States for immediate treatment. I was teaching a workshop in Germany at the time, and before he left for the United States, Jeffrey stopped by to help me in the workshop. When I asked him why he didn't go straight home for treatment, he replied, "What greater healing experience could I have than to be with you and hundreds of people learning the QE process?" As soon as the workshop ended, Jeffrey flew home and submitted himself for treatment.

Jeffrey was admitted into the hospital where his sister works as a nurse. The full severity of his illness was not realized for several days after his admission. The cancer had metastasized throughout his body, including his brain. Once he arrived, he completely let go of any attempt to monitor or interfere with the protocol that was dictated by his doctors. Instead, Jeffrey spent his waking hours frolicking like a child with Eufeeling. In the beginning, the nurses were amazed by Jeffrey's attitude and his nonattachment to the disease that was ravaging his body. As the days rolled by, they became even more amazed by how quickly Jeffrey was healing. They began to call him their sunshine boy and miracle man. Despite the pain and the numbing effect of the medication on body and mind, despite the fact that daily he could see his body wasting away before his eyes, Jeffrey maintained awareness of Eufeeling. He invited the compassion and grace of Eufeeling to enliven his awareness and QE Intention to rejuvenate and revive his body-mind. He did so without any expectation of any results. His motto was, "Eufeeling first, and all else after that."

I am writing this two months after Jeffrey's diagnosis. He is out of the hospital and still under treatment, but he is not out of the woods. Present tests, including spinal puncture, blood tests, and MRIs, show no evidence that the lymphoma exists.

We frequently hear, although not frequently enough, of people healing from serious, life-threatening diseases against all expectations to the contrary. This is not the point I want to make here. Jeffrey's body-mind may still succumb to the cancer. Whether it does or not, Jeffrey's essence, the true Jeffrey, will not. The battle for eternal life has already been won. Jeffrey has transcended the ego-oriented, fear-driven perception that he must control himself and his environment if he is to survive, to be free of suffering. Jeffrey proved there is nowhere to go and nothing to do. Freedom from suffering comes from awareness of Eufeeling, and that can only be had right here, right now.

I want to add a few observations Jeffrey had while going through his ordeal. I think it will help you get a deeper insight into how he perceives his world. I think you will find it refreshing if not healing.

Jeffrey's Insights

- Illness is very cleansing.

- Being removed from the world is not so bad.

- You are never alone . . . there are always the three stooges . . . me, myself, and I . . . and, of course, Eufeeling.

- People love to be thanked, appreciated, and loved.

- Healing is really fun most of the time.

- Good poison (chemotherapy) is sometimes really hard to take.

- The body that I depend on so much is a wrapper for my soul.

- Even when my body is decaying, my spirit does not feel this pain. It feels only sorrow for my body that is suffering. Eufeeling is the resting place of that sorrow.

- The mirror can be a very scary thing with very brutal reflections. It is a good thing that my heart is smiling.

- The person who came up with the saying *bald is beautiful* must have had chemotherapy.

- Ice cream is good.

- Nurses know all the doctors and which ones are the best. Be nice to nurses.

- Being a puppet on strings, with each string being a different drug, makes life interesting to observe, even if it is much more difficult to maneuver.

- Being a passenger in a car, when normally you are the driver, is good practice for letting go of control . . . if you do it enough with bad drivers.

- Ego cannot protect you as much as you may think. Eufeeling, trust, surrender, and love can save you.

- We don't need protection from fear, but we do need protection from people who fear.

Main Points for Chapter 15

- The power and speed with which QE Intention works for chronic sufferers is remarkable. How quickly depends on the type and severity of the sufferer's condition and their constitution.

- Neither you nor QE Intention is the healer. Healing comes out of Eufeeling.

- Whether our partner is healed is not up to us.

- Doing QE Intention for your chronic illness revolves around nonattachment.

- Your illness is perfect just as it is. Denying that means denying the perfection of the present.

- The main component in suffering is not your disease but your perception of it.

- The worst thing you can do to life is attach to death.

- When we have a QE Intention, we forfeit the field of death in favor of the joy of living beyond bounds.

- At no time during QE Intention do we direct energy.

- Freedom from suffering comes from awareness of Eufeeling.

CHAPTER 16

Material Wealth

"He is richest who is content with the least, for content is the wealth of nature."

— SOCRATES

Happiness Is Relative—Eufeeling Is Permanent

When you sit down and think about it, we humans need very little to survive and not much more to make life comfortable. But how much wealth does it take to make us happy? We can answer that question by asking, "How empty does your ego feel?" Our happiness depends on our relative state of affairs. This year, you might be happy to ride a bike to a job you are lucky to have. After a few years of financial success, you might feel bored in a Mercedes. Happiness will always be dependent on relative circumstances, but the need to be happy has a single, constant cause. The spur to greater happiness springs from ego's need to feel full, to reunite with Eufeeling. Striving for material wealth in common consciousness is the outward expression of the ego's inward search for completion. In QE Awareness, one doesn't strive for wealth and isn't dependent on it for happiness. Oddly enough, great wealth often comes to those who are living in accordance with the expression of Eufeeling.

When you are aware of Eufeeling, you have no need to be happy. When you are aware of Eufeeling, you are already at peace with the world. You will naturally do things that make you happy, but you don't need happiness to make you full. Happiness is neither the motivation nor the goal. Those living in QE Awareness who don't amass vast wealth don't need it. That said, there is colossal abundance in this world, and it sure is fun to share in it. There is always a sense of gratitude and awe when we receive a gift given through Eufeeling. One feels that there is a playful impishness working behind the scenes. You don't have the feeling that you earned the gift but that it was given to you for the sheer joy of the giving. Aware of the giver, you are unattached to the gift and can just as easily pass it on to another as keep it for yourself.

The first rule to amass inner or outer wealth is, "Before all else—awareness of Eufeeling." Once you have taken this first step, you have acquired the greatest treasure a human can know: Self-awareness. Settled in the seat of Self, all actions you perform honor and support your Self. From then on, the world is your playground. Having a QE Intention for abundance removes the fear, anxiety, and sense of desperation many have when they deeply desire something. Having a QE Intention is fun. It is accomplished with a sense of playful detachment.

When you have a QE Intention for greater wealth, you will work on two levels: quelling of the emotions attached to the desire and manifestation of the material condition. The emotions that are attached to the object or situation will immediately dissolve into absolute quiescence. There are a wide variety of emotional sharks, swimming around a financial concern. You might recognize them as anxiety or fear, frustration, anger, and confusion. Minutes after having a QE Intention, these emotions, along with their negative influence, will significantly abate or disappear altogether. Free of this emotional bullying, you can sit back and wait for your desire to be fulfilled.

Experience: QE Intention for Material Wealth

Find a comfortable chair where you will not be disturbed for five to ten minutes. Close your eyes, and do the QE process for three to five minutes, or until you feel the quiet presence of Eufeeling. Let your mind go to your desire for greater wealth. For five to ten seconds, watch what your mind shows you about what you want: the fulfillment of that desire. If you have negative emotions attached to your desire for greater wealth, identify them. Let them grow strong and vivid in your mind, and when they are as strong as they can be, grade them from 0 to 10, 10 being unbearable.

Easily allow your mind to return to Eufeeling for a minute or so. After a minute has passed, have the impulse to return to your desire for greater wealth. For the next minute or so, let your mind play the movie about what you want. Your mind may automatically show you a movie of what it is like to have actually achieved your desire. If so, watch the movie, making sure that you don't interfere with the plot. Eufeeling is reorganizing, removing the impediments to the full realization of your desire. After a minute or so, return to Eufeeling.

Repeat the process of revisiting your desire three to five times, making sure to separate each episode with awareness of Eufeeling. If you had negative emotions and did the pretest before your QE Intention session, now is the time to do your posttest. Do exactly as you did at the beginning of the session, and note the strength of your emotions on a scale of 0 to 10. Even in the most desperate cases, we will see significant and immediate dissipation of negative emotions. Many times, negative emotions surrounding financial concerns are more damaging than the actual situation itself. If all we were able to do was eliminate these draining emotions from our financial concerns, that would be worth the price of this book alone. Make sure to take enough time to transition from your quiet state to a state of greater activity by opening and closing your eyes and stretching before you get out of the chair.

Life Is an Easter Egg Hunt

What must you do now to realize your desire of greater wealth? Absolutely nothing! This is perhaps the hardest part for the mind controlled by common consciousness. It will feel that there is a need to do something to make it all work. If you find this to be the case, do QE, and take your common conscious mind to QE Awareness. You will not feel the need to do or to keep checking to see if things are working out. You will have infinite patience, and your patience will be rewarded.

All the organization is being taken care of on the finest and most powerful level of creation. Not much you can do to help out there. However, that does not mean you sit on your thumbs. At this point, you need to be open to opportunities when they present themselves. Stir the pot a little. Think of it like an Easter egg hunt, where Mother Nature has hidden an infinite number of eggs for you to find. Each egg represents the complete fulfillment of your desire, so you only have to find one. Look at each interaction, person, or situation in your life as a bush or a rock that may be hiding your Easter egg. Look for your egg with a sense of ease and playfulness. Meanwhile, make sure that you continue to have a QE Intention session two or three times a day. Happy hunting!

Experience: Helping Others Find Material Wealth

The best way to get is to give. Even if you are wallowing in poverty, you will find immediate inspiration when you have a QE Intention to help someone else find material wealth. Here's how to do it.

Find a comfortable chair where you will not be disturbed for five to ten minutes. Close your eyes, and do the QE process for three to five minutes, or until you feel the quiet presence of Eufeeling. Let your mind go to your partner, the person you want to help. For five to ten seconds, entertain quiet thoughts about how you interpret their problem. If they are suffering, identify their negative emotions as you see them.

Easily shift your awareness from your thoughts about them to Eufeeling. Enjoy the fullness of Eufeeling for a minute or so and then let your thoughts return to your partner. As your mental movie plays, observe your partner to see if they become more acutely aware of their emotions and their physical posture. No matter how they react, as you observe quietly and attentively, become aware of Eufeeling.

Then, like a cat watching a mouse hole, continue to be aware of their body and their emotions and Eufeeling. The stillness or peace or bliss that you are feeling is also alive in them. Observe Eufeeling in your partner for a minute or so, and return to the perception of Eufeeling within yourself.

Alternate between your perception of them and Eufeeling three to five times before ending your QE Intention session. There is no need for you to see them attaining their desire. When you do QE Intention for them, greater material affluence is implied. You are providing the foundation upon which that will happen, but how that happens is not really your concern. You will find great inner satisfaction when doing QE Intention for others' material wealth, and your own efforts to improve your prosperity will also be enhanced. So, make it a habit to help out a friend or two every day. You will be absolutely delighted in your own rewards.

Main Points for Chapter 16

- Our happiness depends on our relative state of affairs.

- When you are aware of Eufeeling, you have no need to be happy.

- QE Intention works on both parts of fulfilling material wealth: the financial situation and the negative emotion attached to it.

- After having a QE Intention, look for opportunities to fulfill your desire.

- Having a QE Intention to help others gain material wealth will also help you.

CHAPTER 17

Problem Solving

"Creativity makes a leap, then looks to see where it is."

— MASON COOLEY

There Are No Problems in Nature

There are no problems in nature. Problems are a man-made phenomenon. They rise out of the human need to impose order on our environment. To the human mind, an orderly environment is one that can be controlled. This order is relative. The degree of disorder depends on the perspective of the observer. The perspective of the observer depends on their perception of harmony. If you perceive your world as a collection of thoughts and things, some of which are related to each other and some are not, you are enjoying the confusion of common consciousness. If, on the other hand, you feel that everything is just right just as it is, you are languishing in QE Awareness.

At its most basic level, Eufeeling only has one moving part. You can't get much more harmonious than that. One cannot be at odds with itself. It takes two to create that phenomenon. When Eufeeling splinters into the infinite shards of creation, the human mind cannot keep track of all that stuff doing all those things. Except in the most limited sense, cause and effect are beyond comprehension. We try, but we are just not capable of knowing everything. Here is where problems are born. Or should I say the illusion of disharmony that we call a problem.

We can't possibly know the result that a single thought or action will have, but still we try. This is where letting go comes in. I don't mean consciously saying something like, "Okay now, Frank, take a deep breath, and just let go." You cannot consciously let go. Conscious effort is still effort, and you cannot make an effort to be effortless. What I'm talking about here is more of an acceptance of what is then a letting go. We cannot accept or believe that everything will be okay when we see that our actions consistently fall short of their mark. We can try to make ourselves believe that we are in control, but that is merely laying one illusion over another. One has to invest a great deal of time and energy into maintaining such a belief.

Acceptance comes naturally from knowing your unbounded, inner Self to be in control. This *knowing* is not an understanding but the deepest intuition that perfection permeates all forms. This realization grows automatically out of the joy, bliss, and love that is you, that is Eufeeling. Any problem has at its roots the ego-oriented, fear-driven perception of the world through common consciousness. And guess what? You can't fix common consciousness with common consciousness. That's like replacing one broken part in a car engine with a different broken part. The engine may function differently, but it will still be broken. Fortunately, common consciousness is easily remedied. You already know how to do it: QE.

So, that takes care of the primal problem of problem solving. But how are we to go about solving specific mysteries, the puzzles that present themselves to us every day? How do we find the time for a vacation when we have already used up all our vacation days? How do we get three kids to three activities in three parts of town at the same time? How do we end a relationship creating as little harm as possible? Why, you already know how to do that as well: QE Intention; QE Intention with a twist.

Experience: Solving Problems with QE Intention

Find a comfortable chair where you will not be disturbed for 10 to 15 minutes. Close your eyes and do the QE process for three to five minutes, or until you feel the quiet fullness of Eufeeling. Now, easily let your mind go to your problem. Take time to review every aspect of your problem. Do not try to solve the problem. This is very important. Only become the perfect observer of the problem as your mind presents it to you. Quietly observe any emotions associated with the problem. Watch them with alert disinterest as they diminish and disappear. Continue to let your mind wander over the various aspects of your problem. Do this for one to three minutes and then easily become aware of Eufeeling.

After a minute or so with Eufeeling, return to pick up the mental threads of your problem movie. Let the thoughts about the problem unfold with you as the interested spectator. Don't be in a hurry, and don't look for a solution. Only be acutely aware of the movie playing on the screen of your mind. Do this for one to three minutes and then return to Eufeeling for a minute or so. Repeat this cycle three to five times. When finished, open your eyes and take time to ease yourself back into activity. Or, if you have the time, remain sitting in your chair, and allow yourself to daydream as long as you feel comfortable doing so.

Traditionally, solutions will come when they are not being looked for. You might find that the answer comes to you just before falling asleep at night or is waiting for you when you wake up in the morning. It may also pop into your mind at any other time during the day, usually during times of reduced concentration, like washing the dishes or driving your car. Give yourself plenty of space, and don't stress to find an answer. You can easily do several sessions of solving problems with QE Intention throughout the day. The best times are first thing in the morning and just before you go to bed at night, but anytime will work just fine.

Main Points for Chapter 17

- There are no problems in nature. Problems are man-made.

- At their foundation, problems are a delusion.

- You cannot make an effort to be effortless.

- You can't fix common consciousness with common consciousness.

- To fix common consciousness, expand it to QE Awareness.

- Traditionally, solutions will come when they are not looked for.

CHAPTER **18**

Saving Your World

"Inventing the future requires giving up control."

— GEORGE LAND

Man Has Lost His Nature

As I begin writing to you this afternoon, I am seated at a desk in a house along a green, sun-dappled valley nestled along the edge of the Black Forest in Kirchzarten, Germany. This house is a wonder to me. It was crafted some 250 years ago, about the time my American fore-fathers, the original supersizers, were making the world's largest cup of tea in Boston Harbor and taking midnight rides to announce the arrival of unwanted guests. Small by today's standards, this two-story home would have been a source of significant pride in this pastoral, Christian, farming community. But the most striking feature of this home is the height of the ceilings and door jams. I am of average height, but I must bow my head, if not reverently then certainly cautiously, when passing from room to room. Once inside a room, I must continue to cast my eyes toward heaven, scouting for low supporting beams that would christen the scalp of a less-weary guest with splintered retribution of an oak felled two and a half centuries before.

Earlier today, I was sitting at a sidewalk café, sipping cappuccino from a white porcelain cup and marveling at the strong, straight bodies of today's Germans. My observation tells me that the present-day German is several inches taller than I. That would make them quite a bit taller than their almost Hobbit-like ancestors.

As I sat and sipped, I wondered if they had cappuccino back then. I found my mind meandering through the streets of the older Kirchzarten. I saw a quieter, less-hectic, more personal time. Harder physically, yes, but softer on the mind. Less clutter, more space for a mind to settle a little before moving on, like a butterfly not a bullet.

By today's standards, Kirchzarten is a quiet but modern village with relatively clean water and air. A good place to convalesce from the endemic outbreak of progress we call New York or Tokyo or Frankfurt. But Kirchzarten is only a relative *eye of the storm*. If the builder of the house were to suddenly appear here next to me in the present-day Kirchzarten town square, his senses would be assaulted by the loud, brash racket of passing cars expelling obnoxious odors, tight-fitting, brightly colored clothes walking and whirring past on bikes, neon signs, vending machines dispensing synthetic sustenance, and tattooed teenagers tapping out text messages on technology that would not even be dreamed of for another 200 years in his Kirchzarten. Can you imagine how he would feel if he were to fly over a major metropolis and look down on rivers of automobiles and seas of humans, spilling into and out of buildings a hundred times taller than his creation? Would he know that as progress?

I began to wonder how the human mind, a child born of and nurtured by nature, has become so utterly alienated from its mother. Even a hundred years ago, man and nature were still friends. Certainly the dreams and aspirations of our ancestors did not include light speed living and mindless multitasking on our way to polluting our planet into extinction.

Transcenders

In every society, there are a few rare individuals who exhibit extraordinary inner harmony. They come in all shapes and sizes and are sometimes impossible to recognize from the rest of us. In his paper "Theory Z," Abraham Maslow, a 20th-century psychologist who studied healthy people, labeled these individuals *transcenders*. Transcenders are not at odds within themselves. They have consciously integrated the outer, chaotic world with an inner coherence that reflects harmony and joy in daily living. Maslow describes transcenders as being in awe of the beauty of even the mundane. They perceive, "sacredness in everyday things." They are intrinsically motivated by truth and beauty and justice, not the fear and greed and need to manipulate that we find so widespread today. Transcenders realize a kind of *oneness* within and express that oneness in their everyday living. They are the ones who naturally live Eufeeling. Their awareness is pure and uncluttered. They see the world with new eyes and are innovators, bringing fresh insights to old dilemmas. Any transcender could sit down and, in 15 minutes, draft a workable solution to world unrest. They see the whole picture and help others place the pieces where they are most needed. In short, transcenders are the hope of the human race. They are the torchbearers who will light the way to inner and outer harmony.

If the torch-bearing transcenders are the saviors of humanity, why aren't they doing their job? Why are we still foundering in this sea of separation? Well, saving the world is no small task. The simple truth is that there are not enough transcenders to get the job done. In short, they need our help, and that is what this book has been about. We are not going to help transcenders; we are going to become transcenders.

Within these pages, you have learned the QE process, how to live QE Awareness, and how to have QE Intention. You have experienced for yourself the speed, simplicity, and gentle power that follow simple awareness of Eufeeling. You now have the technology to fulfill any and all of your desires while, at the same time and without effort, increasing harmony and peace in our world. You, like Maslow's transcenders, have become a torchbearer, dispelling the shadows of disharmony within and without. Now that you know the subtle secret of Eufeeling, no one can take it away from you.

Cities and countries, political organizations, religions, universities, and corporations are all made of individuals. They are the reflection of the collective thinking of those individuals. On every level of collective human existence, there is conflict. No matter how well-meaning the motivation—save the whales, urban renewal, or even world peace—it is sure to find opposition. Conflict between groups of individuals is the direct reflection of the conflict within the individual. No proclamation of world peace, no matter how lofty the organization that crafts it, can secure world peace. World peace will be realized only when the individuals of that world are at peace within themselves. Efforts on behalf of world peace begin with hope and eventually dissolve into disillusionment. It is not that the problem of world peace is too big or too complicated. It is that our efforts have led us in the opposite direction from success. The solution to world disharmony is not only attainable, it is simple, exciting, and fun. We have everything we need to establish world peace right now, right here, within each and every one of us. Here's what I mean.

Peace Is Now

A scientific phenomenon called the n^2 effect makes true peace on a global scale a realistic goal. When the square root of one percent of a population becomes coherent, that coherency creates a phase transition within that population, which results in complete coherence. That is to say, if you have the square root of one percent of, let's say photons for instance, vibrating at the same frequency, they will have a harmonizing influence on the other discordant photons. The square root of one percent of the photons of an incandescent light can cause dissonant photons to vibrate at the same frequency, creating more harmony, focus, and power. Another name for this coherent light is laser light. The same is true with humans. The square root of one percent marching in step will get all of the others to march to the beat of that same drum.

Someone like a transcender, someone living in QE Awareness who has left common consciousness behind, has a powerful harmonizing influence on their environment. When two or more are gathered together, their influence is squared. That means when two people in QE Awareness are together, they have the harmonizing power of four people in QE Awareness, four people together in QE Awareness have the organizing influence of 16, 16 people create the equivalent of 256 people, 256 people equal 65,536 people. and so on. This phenomenon is vividly demonstrated during QE workshops, when we have hundreds of people experiencing QE Awareness for a whole weekend. It is a window into the future of humankind . . . that is, if we can pull it off, if we can inspire enough people to become transcender-like inhabitants of this beautifully rich world our earth is providing for us.

Because of the n^2 effect that people in QE Awareness have on their surroundings, it only takes the square root of one percent of a population to create a phase transition. In other words, the square root of the population living QE Awareness will positively influence how the rest of the people in that city live even if they aren't aware of the transcender-like people in their midst. That is an amazingly small number. One percent for a city of one million people is one thousand people. The square root of 1,000 people is 32 people! It would only take 32 people in QE Awareness to create an uplifting, harmonizing, and healing effect on a city of one million people.

This principle was tested by Transcendental meditators in the 1960s and 1970s, measuring the FBI's crime rate statistics. Crime rate was decreased an average of 24 percent in 22 major cities in the United States when the square root of one percent of the city's population was matched by transcender-like meditators. If we want to immediately create a healthier, cleaner, more productive, and loving life for all the inhabitants of the United States, it will only take 1,760 transcenders like you living in Eufeeling. To have peace and prosperity spread throughout the world, we will only need a little more than 8,000 people in QE Awareness!

The really neat thing is you don't have to concern yourself with world peace. You don't even have to believe it can happen. You can be quite self-centered—or, more accurately, Self-centered—about this whole thing if you like, and we will all still benefit. You could live in a cave in QE Awareness, and the rest of us human iron filings would begin to organize around your coherency. It's simple quantum mechanics. It is the way we humans were meant to work.

That is why I have written this book. Our focus is not on world peace but individual peace. That makes world peace personal. We don't have to join groups, write documents, or foster hope and belief that world peace will someday materialize. We only have to find peace within, and it will naturally radiate outward, warming our world to its influence. Even if you've tried to be peaceful before and failed, you don't have to worry. This is new technology founded on principles as old as consciousness itself. QE and QE Intention work when we stop working, when we are still in the pure awareness of Eufeeling. Awareness of Eufeeling is sublime. It is the birthright of every human being on this earth, and it is working its way into the hearts and harmony of humankind around the world. Its name is strange, but its practice is as familiar as the rhythmic beating of your heart. Eufeeling is a warm and welcoming light. Its soft, inviting glow re-assures you of the safety and comfort waiting within. Reunited with your Self, you heave a great sigh as the mantle of the world's worries falls effortlessly from your shoulders. You are free. Welcome home.

Appendix

The Quantum Entrainment Triangulation Technique

Healing with QE is actually realizing that you are not healing. You are not creating positive energy to overcome negative energy. You are not calling on other forces or formulas to do your bidding. You *are* creating an atmosphere in which healing will take place. QE is tapping into the field (for lack of a better word) of perfect order. From there, you do nothing, and everything gets done for you.

As a matter of convention, I will say, "You heal," or, "I healed," but that is not strictly true. In preparation for creating a healing event, we must adopt the correct angle of entry to be successful. For me to say that we do not perform the healing is neither attitude nor philosophy. It is a simple fact based on observation. This healing presence is not a foreign force that is beyond you but your very own essence—pure awareness reflected through Eufeeling. Nothing more, nothing less.

You will be amazed by the power your awareness holds, but know that you do not own that power. You are that power and will soon experience it firsthand. You will slip beyond the boundaries that you have meticulously built these past decades in order to define the little you. These boundaries have confined your awareness to thoughts and things that have served to strengthen your concept of *me*. However, that will be set aside the very first time you experience QE.

Now, let's roll up our sleeves and get ready to create a healing event. We'll start with a simple case: a friend has asked you to help him with left shoulder pain and muscle tension in the upper back and neck. With QE, it is not necessary to know the cause of the condition. Healing will take place on the causal level automatically. As the initiator, you only need to know what is desired. Obviously, your partner desires relief from his shoulder pain and muscle tension. That is inferred and is also your intention. It is all the info you need.

Getting Ready to Heal

Before you start, have your partner move his shoulder so that it creates the pain he wants to eliminate. Have him show you how his range of motion is diminished and anything else that demonstrates how the body is affected by this condition. Then ask him to grade the severity of his pain on a scale of 1 to 10 (10 being unbearable), and note that number. It's also important to get into the habit of pretesting and posttesting. This will give you valuable feedback, especially in the beginning, when you are just getting used to the QE process. If you are a physician, use the same tests you would employ for traditional treatment. For instance, a chiropractor might use orthopedic and neurological tests, palpation, and even x-rays to objectively identify the problem and determine the level of improvement.

You only need to be aware of the intention one time. Pure awareness is neither deaf nor dumb. It will know what you want better than you will. Pure awareness will know what to do and when to do it—of this you can be sure. Now you are ready to start.

Triangulation: The Three-Step QE Process

On your partner's shoulder, upper back, or neck, it should be easy to find a muscle that is tight or painful to the touch. Place the tip of your index finger (Contact A) on a tight muscle. Push in firmly so that you can feel how hard or tense the muscle is. Then relax, and let your finger rest lightly on the tight muscle. Now, lightly place the index finger of your other hand (Contact B) on any other muscle. It does not have to be taut or sore to the touch. Just pick a muscle at random, and place your finger there.

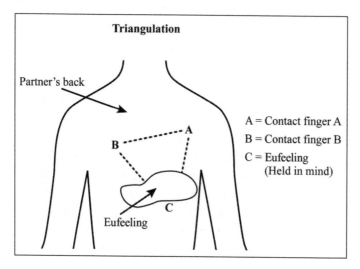

185

QE Triangulation Healing Technique

Step 1: Focus all of your attention on Contact A, and become very aware of what you feel. Take the time to notice the heat from the muscle on the tip of your finger, the texture of your partner's skin or clothing, the tightness of the muscle pushing back against your finger, and so on. Become aware of everything you can where finger and muscle meet. Do this for 10 to 15 seconds.

Step 2: Become acutely aware of Contact B, just as you did with Contact A. Then become clearly aware of what both fingers are feeling *at the same time.* Maintain this awareness for several seconds. While you simultaneously hold your attention on both fingers, you will also notice a separate part of you that is just watching the whole process take place. You, your awareness, is aware of both fingers. So far, you have awareness of Contact A, awareness of Contact B, and awareness that you are aware of both at the same time. It doesn't matter if you are clearly aware of this phenomenon; it is happening naturally, without effort.

Step 3: As you hold awareness of the two points in this expanded way, do nothing. That's right—just pay attention to what you are sensing in the tips of your two fingers, and that is all. If you are simultaneously paying attention to your two contact fingers and doing nothing else, you will soon begin to feel a sense of quietness, stillness, or even peace. This is a Eufeeling generated from your expanded awareness. At this point, become aware of this sensation as you hold your awareness on Contacts A and B.

You now have three points of awareness: Contact A, Contact B, and your Eufeeling. Holding them in your awareness is called *triangulation*. Continue to be aware of all three points until you feel a change in your partner's body, particularly in his muscles. (This can take several minutes when you are first learning QE.) The change you experience might be a softening or loosening of the muscles under your fingers. It may feel as if your fingers are relaxing or dissolving into the muscles themselves. Or you may feel that your partner is generally relaxing. His shoulders might loosen, or he may sigh or take a deeper breath. If you are both standing, you might note that your partner is swaying. This is a common reaction to the very deep level of healing rest that your partner is enjoying. You may also notice that your partner is generating more body heat or even sweating.

Any one of these changes signify that your partner's body is healing. It is reorganizing to eliminate the disorderly pain and tension. After you observe any of these indicators, continue to triangulate by simultaneously being aware of the two contact points and your Eufeeling a little while longer. Then remove your fingers.

Congratulations! You have just completed your first QE session. With just two fingers and your Eufeeling, you have eliminated your partner's suffering!

You might be wondering what your partner is experiencing while you are creating this healing event. The answer is absolutely nothing. Before a QE session begins, I tell my partner, "Just let your mind wander wherever it wants to go." I am often asked by partners if they should relax, meditate, or repeat their own intention. They should do *nothing*. They should not try to help in any way, because if they do, it would only slow down or counteract the initiator's efforts. The reason for this is since their minds are busy with other chores, they are less open to the healing influence that QE generates. However, a mind in "neutral" will naturally and effortlessly drop into the healing waters of pure awareness.

Always make your partners comfortable. If they wish, they can close their eyes, but that is all the preparation they need. If they want to help you in some way, you can tell them that the best thing they can do is to allow their mind to wander with no direction or intent.

QE works very well under the most trying circumstances. Your partner may be in a great deal of physical or emotional pain. You may find yourself performing QE in an emergency room, a crowded mall, or in any other unsettling environment; and healing will still take place. So, don't think that you are limited by these things. But given the choice, a serene environment with a compliant partner is always preferable.

The QE Session in a Nutshell

- Partner describes pain (intention implied).
- Pretest.
- Become aware of Contact A (hard or painful muscle).
- Become aware of Contact B.
- Become aware of both A and B at the same time.
- Wait for Eufeeling.
- Hold awareness of A, B, and Eufeeling.

- Observe partner's muscles relaxing, body swaying, breathing changes, or other signs of relaxation.
- Posttest.

❦

Glossary

Common Consciousness: Consciousness unaware of Self, of Eufeeling. Common consciousness is subservient to the fear and prejudice of ego; generally destructive, even when intentions are positive. One feels that they are the initiator of their actions, that they are the creator of things and thoughts. The prevalent form of consciousness in the world. The opposite of *QE Awareness*.

Ego: The loss of awareness of Eufeeling, resulting in the illusion of individuality. It is the controlling entity of the unaware mind. Ego is born of fear, which is both its foil and its fuel. It wants to be whole and merge with Eufeeling but fears assimilation by it. Ego tries to eliminate what it cannot control. It feels that if it can control everything, it can be whole. It is the primal cause of suffering. Time, fear, and ego are one and the same. Ego is an illusion. QE Awareness eliminates ego's destructive influence over the mind not by destroying it but by expanding it to infinity.

Eufeeling: Eufeeling ("euphoric feeling") is a perception of wholeness, of the first glimmering of awareness in the mind. The natural state of human awareness. Eufeeling is timeless and cannot die. The mind recognizes Eufeeling as pure peace, stillness, joy, compassion, love, bliss, and so forth. The lens through which pure awareness creates. The foundation for QE Awareness. *Eufeeling* and *Self* are synonymous.

Mistake of the Ego: The false ides that ego can fill the void left by separation from Eufeeling by filling its existence with material things, mental concepts, and the play of emotions. Movement of the mind outward, away from Eufeeling.

Pure Awareness: Awareness of that which is unchanging, without beginning or end. Awareness of nothing. The state of no thoughts; the gap. One is not aware of pure awareness while it is happening. Beyond energy and form. Every created thing is the unmoving, non-existent illusion of pure awareness.

Pure Eufeeling: The perception of Eufeeling before it takes form in the mind. The experience of awareness of pure awareness while remaining aware; not thought, not feeling, but still aware. The state from which miracles are created. Spontaneous materialization of corporeal form like the fishes and the loaves, sacred ash, instantaneous healing of disease. The purest state of individual awareness.

Quantum Entrainment (QE): The effortless process of guiding common consciousness to pure awareness and then anchoring it in Eufeeling. QE is successful when it stops working in pure awareness.

QE Awareness: Action performed while aware of Eufeeling. Awareness beyond the bonds of cause and effect, free of fear and disharmony. One becomes the observer as creation takes place through them, not from them. The opposite of *Common Consciousness*.

QE Intention: The effortless fulfillment of desire while aware of Eufeeling. Immediately resolves emotional disharmony and attachment to desire, while organizing the forces of creation around satisfying the desire on the material plane. Fulfillment of the primal, deepest desire to be reunited with inner Self, free of fear. Desiring without ego. Always gives more than is asked for. Creates from perfect harmony. Cannot oppose the basic creative forces. Can do no harm.

Self: See *Eufeeling*.

Self-Awareness: See *QE Awareness*.

About the Author

Dr. Frank J. Kinslow has been researching and teaching healing techniques for more than 35 years. He draws from his clinical experience as a chiropractic physician, in-depth studies into Eastern esoteric philosophies and practices, and an ardent love of relativity and quantum physics. In 2007, the Quantum Entrainment process of instant healing was born out of a personal crisis that left Dr. Kinslow with *nowhere to go and nothing to do.* Out of this *nothing,* he was able to create a vibrant and fulfilling life for himself. He began to teach and write with such simplicity and clarity that in just a few years, tens of thousands of people around the world were able to create vibrant and fulfilling lives for themselves just by reading his books.

Dr. Kinslow is a chiropractic physician, a teacher for the deaf, and a Doctor of Clinical Spiritual Counseling. He continues to write and teach extensively. He resides in Sarasota, Florida, with his wife, Martina.

Website: **www.QuantumEntrainment.com**

About the QE Organization

Dr. Kinslow is the originator and sole teacher of Quantum Entrainment. He conducts seminars and lectures worldwide. For more information about QE, please contact the organization:

Website: **www.QuantumEntrainment.com**
E-mail: **Info@QuantumEntrainment.com**
Phone: (877) 811-5287 (toll-free in North America)

QE Products

Books

The Secret of Instant Healing
The Secret of Quantum Living
Beyond Happiness: Finding and Fulfilling Your Deepest Desire

Audio Books

The Secret of Instant Healing
The Secret of Quantum Living

Eufeeling! The Art of Creating Inner Peace and Outer Prosperity

Beyond Happiness: Finding and Fulfilling Your Deepest Desire

CDs

Exercises for Quantum Living (2-CD set)
Exercises for Quantum Living for Two (2-CD set)
Quantum Entrainment Exercises

DVDs

Quantum Entrainment Introductory Presentation
What the Bleep QE Video

Other Services Found at **www.QuantumEntrainment .com**:

- Private Sessions from Certified QE Specialists

- The QE Quill [Free] Newsletter

- Free Downloads

- QE Videos and Pictures

- The QE Forum

❧ NOTES ❧

❧ NOTES ❧

❧ NOTES ❧

Hay House Titles of Related Interest

YOU CAN HEAL YOUR LIFE, the movie,
starring Louise L. Hay & Friends
(available as a 1-DVD program and an expanded 2-DVD set)
Watch the trailer at: **www.LouiseHayMovie.com**

THE SHIFT, the movie, starring Dr. Wayne W. Dyer
(available as a 1-DVD program and an expanded 2-DVD set)
Watch the trailer at: **www.DyerMovie.com**

❧

AWAKENING THE LUMINOUS MIND: Tibetan Meditation
for Inner Peace and Joy, by Tenzin Wangyal Rinpoche

BREAKING THE HABIT OF BEING YOURSELF: How to
Lose Your Mind and Create a New One, by Dr. Joe Dispenza

HEART THOUGHTS: A Treasury of Inner Wisdom,
by Louise L. Hay

THE MINDFUL MANIFESTO: How Doing Less and Noticing
More Can Help Us Thrive in a Stressed-Out World,
by Dr. Jonty Heaversedge & Ed Halliwell

9 DAYS TO FEEL FANTASTIC: How to Create Happiness
from the Inside Out, by John Whiteman

SOUL-CENTERED: Transform Your Life in 8 Weeks
with Meditation, by Sarah McLean

All of the above are available at your local bookstore,
or may be ordered by contacting Hay House (see next page).

❧

We hope you enjoyed this Hay House book. If you'd like to receive our online catalog featuring additional information on Hay House books and products, or if you'd like to find out more about the Hay Foundation, please contact:

Hay House, Inc., P.O. Box 5100, Carlsbad, CA 92018-5100
(760) 431-7695 or (800) 654-5126
(760) 431-6948 (fax) or (800) 650-5115 (fax)
www.hayhouse.com® • **www.hayfoundation.org**

✲

Published and distributed in Australia by: Hay House Australia Pty. Ltd., 18/36 Ralph St., Alexandria NSW 2015 • *Phone:* 612-9669-4299 *Fax:* 612-9669-4144 • www.hayhouse.com.au

Published and distributed in the United Kingdom by: Hay House UK, Ltd., 292B Kensal Rd., London W10 5BE • *Phone:* 44-20-8962-1230 • *Fax:* 44-20-8962-1239 • www.hayhouse.co.uk

Published and distributed in the Republic of South Africa by: Hay House SA (Pty), Ltd., P.O. Box 990, Witkoppen 2068 *Phone/Fax:* 27-11-467-8904 • www.hayhouse.co.za

Published in India by: Hay House Publishers India, Muskaan Complex, Plot No. 3, B-2, Vasant Kunj, New Delhi 110 070 • *Phone:* 91-11-4176-1620 • *Fax:* 91-11-4176-1630 • www.hayhouse.co.in

Distributed in Canada by: Raincoast, 9050 Shaughnessy St., Vancouver, B.C. V6P 6E5 • *Phone:* (604) 323-7100 *Fax:* (604) 323-2600 • www.raincoast.com

✲

Take Your Soul on a Vacation

Visit **www.HealYourLife.com®** to regroup, recharge, and reconnect with your own magnificence. Featuring blogs, mind-body-spirit news, and life-changing wisdom from Louise Hay and friends.

Visit **www.HealYourLife.com** today!

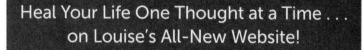